POLITICIANS
WITHOUT BORDERS

How the Far Right and the Far
Left Keep Screwing It Up for All
of Us in the Far Center

"Cell tower down again!"

JOHN P. BROACH

authorHOUSE®

AuthorHouse™
1663 Liberty Drive
Bloomington, IN 47403
www.authorhouse.com
Phone: 1 (800) 839-8640

Published by AuthorHouse   09/01/2015

ISBN: 978-1-5049-2492-4 (sc)
ISBN: 978-1-5049-2491-7 (e)

Previous publications

Playing Politics from the Left and the Right

DEDICATION

To:

VanJohLin

"YOU KNOW WHO YOU ARE"

ACKNOWLEDGMENTS

Art provided by Mathew McFarren.

CONTENTS

ADVICE TO READERS xi

CENTER PIECE 1 1

THE UNITED STATES SUPREME COURT 1
"Nine Lawyers Who Can't Agree On One Piece Of
Paper Written In English"

CENTER PIECE 2 18

THE UNITED NATIONS 18
"To Meet A Lot/To Disagree A Lot/ To Spend A Lot"

CENTER PIECE 3 32

THE ELECTORAL COLLEGE 32
"Your Vote Doesn't Count'

CENTER PIECE 4 44

VICE PRESIDENTS, FIRST LADIES AND
SECOND PLACE 44
"Is There Any Difference?'

THE LITERARY SORBET 55

READER: COLLECT YOUR THOUGHTS
You're Now Smarter Than 80% Of The Electorate

CENTER PIECE 5..60

**POLITICAL COMMENTARY WHERE
QUALITY IS JOB ELEVEN** 60
"As Brought To You By: The Self Anointed/ The
Self Appointed/ And The Self Absorbed"

CENTER PIECE 6..77

THE FEDERAL RESERVE SYSTEM (FED)..............77
"We Speak Only In Tongues'

CENTER PIECE 7.. 88

THE FBI / THE CIA / THE IRS....................................88
"We're On Top Of Everything-Especially You"

CENTER PIECE DE RESISTANCE
(*That's #8, Dummy*)..100

**THE PEACE CHAMPIONSHIP SERIES (PCS)
DEFEATS WAR**
"Drafting From The Popularity Of The American
College Bowl Championship Series (BCS), War Is
Compressed To One Match Per Year. Winner Take
All! Grieve And Heal"

ADVICE TO READERS

This Section of a book is usually called a Prologue. But nobody ever reads a Prologue because it's not interesting and you never get tested on the material in it.

Since Prologue doesn't work for us, we have chosen to call this Section *Advice to Readers*. 'Advice to Readers' is the literary equivalent of "individual results may vary." For example, the author of this book has a sense of humor and correctly reckons that the majority of folks do not live their lives in the hardened bunkers of narrow, ideological thought (i.e., Washington D.C.). This is called, 'being normal'. The author also recognizes that because we are a country of **participation not partition**, we come from a broad spectrum of race and ethnicity, and therefore it is okay to have a differing view without being Al Qaeda or even Al Sharpton.

We don't have Chapters in this book—we have *Center Pieces*. In addition we strongly believe that if there can be a Far Right and a Far Left—there can and should be, a Far Center (therefore the name 'Center Piece'). If you will recall, a Center Piece was that thoughtful floral arrangement your mom placed in the middle of the dinner table when you were growing up, over and around which you hurled insult and invective in the guise of a family conversation about politics.

Perhaps a moment of explanation would be helpful here. The **Far Right** is defined as those people who believe that mainstream, moderate political thought is uninformed and dangerous. The **Far Left** is defined as those people who believe mainstream, moderate political thought is uninformed and boorish. The **Far Center** (gasp) believes in mainstream, moderate political thought!

The Far Center further distinguishes itself from the Far Left because we are presently not **grieving, outraged or healing**. These three elements are central to the Far Left in order for them to lionize a lame thought; demonize a conservative; or memorialize the forgettable, (e.g. anything that has happened in Hollywood). In contrast, the Far Center is wholly separate from the Far Right because we don't like **organized religion** because we're afraid we might pick the wrong scripture; we don't believe in **nation-building**, in the name of democracy, because our country always picks the wrong side and further that there are two sides to each coin, unless it's in Karl Rove's pocket.

Since the business of this book is to enjoy, not ridicule, we will not be ad hominem, not ad wominem (?!) and definitely not ad nauseum. We reserve the right to make fun of **everyone** and particularly every stereotype generated by the Far Left (the self-anointed), the Far Right (the self-appointed), and those people who actually believe them (the self-deluded). The best way for you to participate in this fun, **and prepare to cast a knowledgeable vote**, for the person you least dislike in any political election, is to examine the institutions on which our political system is based.

This book is also introducing three new concepts to the bloated body politic and its' tedious political participants: 1) we will be factual 2) we will be informative and 3) we will be funny. If you watch past Presidential debates, you can see that my concept hasn't fully caught on yet.

Finally, **alert to readers!** This is the first publication of any kind with a literary *'Sorbet'*. Located between Center Pieces 4 and 5, the Sorbet will give you a chance to use the crayons that the bookstore gave you in order to bribe you to buy this book. If you don't know what a Sorbet is—look it up. Now please read on, so that your vote will be the most informed one to be lost in your State.

CENTER PIECE 1

The United States Supreme Court

Motto: "We Are Separated by One Piece of Paper and a Common Cause. What would You Expect of Nine Lawyers?"

Why do we have a Supreme Court?

The Founding Fathers knew that U.S. Presidents would come and go and that mercifully, Vice Presidents would mostly go. However, some institutions deserved to be around a lot. That's the reason they invented the U.S. Supreme Court. In addition, since we are a country of laws, we needed a law mechanism to put an end to protracted disputes, **today**, so that we can elect a new set of politicians who will bring new protracted disputes before us, **tomorrow**. This is how the system works. Over 40 years ago, a guy in Arizona was convicted of rape and kidnapping and he gave the cops a confession because he was guilty as hell, and he got convicted and was sentenced to 20-30 years. But later he got a very clever attorney who went to the Supreme Court and said this guy was such a moron that he should have kept his mouth shut and a good lawyer, like himself, could have gotten this societal canker-sore off for less time in jail. The Supreme Court agreed, the guy got a new trial and he ended up doing 11 years. (This case will be discussed later). Why is this important? Exactly the point, **it isn't important anymore!** Nobody can afford a lawyer. So you end up getting a court appointed guy who gets you 11 years in the slam.

But now we have **new** politicians who think **new** things are important. Such things as, torturing people in Guantanamo Bay who probably deserve it; treating native Americans like hell who never deserved it; health care for everybody; and letting illegal immigrants remain in our country doing crappy jobs so that real Americans can continue in poverty entitlement programs.

The Far Left and the Far Right absolutely love the Supreme Court. It is the most yeasty soil in the entire American system, in which to seed their bromides of extremism. *(Reader Alert: You will learn many new words and phrases in this book. 'bromides of extremism' is just one of them. It doesn't mean much, but in a heated political exchange, launching these words at your adversary will stop him in his tracks and make you appear wizened).*

I now have an unquenchable thirst for knowledge of the Supreme Court. Please tell me about its historical beginnings!

The Supreme Court was formed in 1790. It originally had only six justices, none of whose names are important or memorable so I'm not going to discuss them. What is important, is that for the first 145 years (1790 to 1935) of its existence, the court didn't have its own *pied a terre* (French for "hood"). The justices were itinerant types who scoured the land for landmark decisions to make. But this had its problems. Because they were always on the road these guys never had a chance to get together and furrow their respective brows and give each other furtive looks. And believe me, if you're a lawyer, this is important stuff. So they all decided, "Hey, we're in New York City already, it's a cool place, Des Moines hasn't been founded yet, unless anybody has a better idea let's just stay here?" This was historical. It was the first unanimous Supreme Court agreement, and was one of very few after that.

No sooner had these boys gotten snugly ensconced in the Big Apple, than the U.S. government decided to move to Philadelphia, Pennsylvania. You can't be important (Supreme) if all the action is in Philly and you're in New York City. So the court tagged along to Philadelphia. Once in Philadelphia, the court signed a long-term lease at Independence Hall. This seemed to be just perfect for them. Centrally located downtown, within easy walking distance to famous Revolutionary War stuff, and quite handsome for Philadelphia. But "the super" at Independence Hall was a little short on tolerance and quickly tired of these guys screaming out in pig Latin and running around in their robes at all hours. So the Supremes packed up their gavels and headed across town to City Hall, where they felt more welcome and could play to a larger house.

No sooner had they picked out the curtains than the Government was on the move again—this time to Washington, D.C. So off to D.C. they go, valise in hand, declining Latin nouns on their way. When they got to D.C., things went from bad to worse. At least in Philadelphia they had a permanent place to be thrown out of. In Washington, D.C., they had to shuffle around the Capitol Building from one room to another. This is probably why the Supreme Court, to this day, takes a three-month recess—it takes them that long to find each other.

What could possibly be next? We'll tell you what's next. The British torched the Capitol Building in the War of 1812, and these poor bastards were on the street, again. By now, they'd moved so many times that The *New York Times* began referring to them as The Supreme Schleps. Anyway, guess what happened next? Nothing! They hung around in D.C. for more than 100 years and in 1935 landed some good digs, in their own building, and they've been there ever since. The building's architecture is compelling, historical, enlightening, and all that stuff. Therefore I have devoted one sentence to it—later.

Now that these guys get moved in and take some time to catch up on their reading: they start to turn the Constitution of the United States every which way but loose. Some of the justices even read it **twice**. I don't know if you are aware of this, but the Supremes have no other real function than to be the final word in controversies where the "application and interpretation of the Constitution" (The Real Big C) are required. That's their total job description. So now we have nine guys with four clerks each (a total of 45 folks) and only two jobs—applying and interpreting the Constitution. **And they still can't agree!**

All this notwithstanding, Alex de Tocqueville, the famous French philosopher (and the last Frenchman to like us) described the Supreme Court, over 150 years ago, as a classic example of "American exceptionalism." Imagine that! About the same time, the French also gave us the Statue of Liberty. Back in those days we must have been very exceptional.

All that may have been fine 150 years ago, but according to both the Far Right and the Far Left, it's been pretty much downhill from there. The folks on both the left and the right believe that recent Supreme Court decisions around obscenity, sex, same sex, same old sex, etc., seem to have moved this institution from the **venerable** to the **venereal**! As if this alone were not cause enough for fulmination and aggressive hand gesturing, things have gotten even worse. Since 1973, the Court has heard over 60 cases involving abortion, family planning, and obscenity. Those of us who would just rather see a good water-rights fight or a bitter imminent-domain skirmish see a disturbing pattern emerging when one of the most important parts of the "body political" (the Supreme Court) is forced to deal with one of the most controversial parts of the "body anatomical" (the genitals).

Perhaps these issues of abortion and obscenity are important today (or perhaps not), but let's remember: the founders of the country hadn't even heard of these types of problems 200 years ago. In the 1700s, when the Constitution was written, planned parenthood meant marrying an ugly girl. And since Justice Potter Stewart hadn't been born yet, the Founders didn't have the benefit of his clarity when, in 1967, he said of obscenity: "I don't know how to define it, but I know it when I see it!" Wow! Think where we'd be today if the Founders had quit dithering with equality and representation and freedom and other pursuits and had instead buckled down to the task of frontal and backal nudity. I'm surprised the French don't like us even more today.

Irrespective of the nature of decisions the Supreme Court makes, it never decides anything that isn't labeled "milestone" or "landmark." We know this because that's what we're told. I, for one, don't feel all that mile-stoned or land-marked. For example, in Miranda v. Arizona, the Court decided that if you get arrested you have the right to have someone read your rights to you. (Rights are one of those things the Founders wasted time on instead of obscenity.) I don't have the numbers at my fingertips, but I have a feeling that 99.5 percent of all Americans go through life without ever being arrested. So except for Ernesto Miranda and his buddies, this weighty court decision is not going to help out the folks much. How about Roe v. Wade (that abortion thing again)? Once more, if 99.5 percent of all Americans go through life without an abortion, then could someone please tell me why it's so important and why we get so excited about the .5 percent? (I really do know the answer to that question. The Far Right believes abortion is all about God. The Far Left believes it's all about a woman's right to choose. Those of us in the Far Center believe that if it is all about choosing and all about God, then choose a different God. Problem solved!) Assuming that nobody jumps on the Far Center's idea, we are going to have to worry about this subject forever because the Far Left and the Far Right say we should. (In the "Sorbet," you will be given the opportunity to identify Jane Roe's real name and what this dude Wade was all about [true]).

Although these things seem to be negative and distant, the Supreme Court often takes some time in its busy schedule to be relevant. Brown v. Board of Education (Topeka, Kansas) is a notable example. In 1954—and almost exclusively because the Founding Fathers had spent too much time on "Rights" and not enough time on "Obscenity," the court was faced with the problem of whether or not to desegregate the entire American school system. With uncharacteristic resolve, to say nothing of the last time they all agreed on something, they voted that "separate but equal" just didn't cut it anymore. Although the case had absolutely no legal basis in the Constitution and was a blatant example of judicial activism, it endures to this day as one of the court's finer decisions and is the strongest indication that these court guys can do fine work if they're well rested.

The Supreme Court building

As I said, we're going to spend a little time on the court building and its architecture. The building came in almost $10 million (in 1935 dollars) under budget! That's the reason it has been populated mostly by Republicans since then. The architect was a guy named Gilbert. Guess who Gilbert was friends with? Mussolini! (True). That's whom he got the Italian marble from to make all those columns. I'm trying to be outraged—are you?

The front of the court has 12 marble columns, which hold up the pediment. The pediment is the first thing you see when you walk up the Supreme Court steps (unless Alan

Dershowitz is outside eating a hoagie). As you can see, the pediment shows lots of people doing things that are very hard to understand. Inside the court building is the impediment. You can't see it, but trust me, that's where lots of people—otherwise known as the Supreme Court justices—are doing things that are very hard to understand.

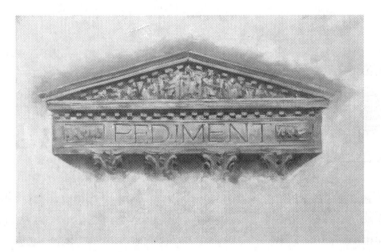

The Nine Supreme Court Justices

Selection to the Supreme Court

Each U.S. President is allowed to nominate a justice when a vacancy occurs. Allowable vacancies are considered death, or inconclusive carbon dating" results. Unallowable vacancies are senility. The legal term for the process of nominating justices is called "stacking the bench." Once the President of the United States (POTUS) has nominated a justice to the Supreme Court of the United States (SCOTUS), it is the avowed duty of the opposing political party to make each nominee wish they had died at birth (CORPUS). Treating a nominee to the Supreme Court in this manner is called a "Bork Job" after Robert Bork, who was a nominee to the Court but who **didn't** get confirmed.

Bork was a heavy in the Nixon administration and was also the guy who fired Special Prosecutor Archibald Cox, who was asking Nixon questions about Watergate tapes and White House plumbers. (Please note: In the "Sorbet," you will be given the chance to identify why they were called the "White House plumbers").

Anyway, let's continue. Archibald Cox, if you will remember, was the guy who thought it would be in the country's best interest to take a little peek at those Watergate tapes. Well, during Bork's confirmation process things got out of hand fast. Bork was repeatedly and rudely asked why he fired Archibald Cox just because Arch repeatedly and rudely demanded that then President Nixon turn over those pesky Watergate tapes. Senator Edward Kennedy of Massachusetts led the assault on Bork and did so with such fervor and righteous indignation that he clean forgot to notice that the hearings had gone on well into the cocktail hour and had to be reminded by his staff of his priorities. Remember in the beginning I told you that 13 nominees had not made the cut? Guess who **was** No. 13? Although Bork was an exception, in most instances once a nominee's reputation and life have been ruined he/she is confirmed as a justice.

Our current Supreme Court has five justices who were nominated by Republican Presidents and four by Democratic Presidents. Normally you would think that the court would therefore "dress to the right." Somehow or other, it hasn't seemed to always work that way. Apparently the justices lie convincingly at their confirmation hearings (known as a "Blow Job" after Bork's "blown" opportunity to lie better and blame everything he did on someone else), because once these guys get on the bench they immediately cop an attitude and start letting their conscience and the Constitution rule their decisions. Imagine the gall! So be it—we live with unfairness daily! However, the Far Right is far from amused. As a matter of fact, Pat Robertson, religious bon vivant and standard-bearer for tolerance **in moderation**, feels that some of the court's decisions have moved so far to the Far Left, that perhaps divine intervention may be required to correct a runaway situation. To wit (legal for **to wit**) he has asked God to visit a few of the justices in a dream and ask them to die! This is a thoughtful—and clearly no fingerprints—solution, but those of us in the Far Center are not sure this is what the Framers of the Constitution had in mind.

How are Supreme Court decisions really made?

We now know there are nine justices $(5 + 4 = 9)$; therefore, no case ever has to go to sudden death due to a tie. In addition, instant replay to overturn a decision made by the justices requires three-fourths' approval of all state legislatures. Finally, as we mentioned before, all decisions made by the

Court are **landmark**. This means that they are so important that only the Supreme Court could make them. Again evidence of the wisdom of the Founding Fathers who would be damned if they were going to give these guys a cushy job and then **not** get "landmark" stuff from their rulings. You might be interested to know that lower courts are also allowed to make "mark" decisions. Federal, state, and traffic courts make "hash," "pock" and "skid" decisions in that order.

By and large, the court's decisions achieve milestone historical status, are wide sweeping, and in comparison to the make-up of our population, affect almost no one. Those of us in the Far Center refer to these decisions as **decisis onanismus**.

This notwithstanding, the decision process is rigorous and involves the justices reading "briefs," listening to oral arguments, pointing menacingly at each other, pouting, and then finally making up their minds (called **deciding**). It's hard to make this process fun, but occasionally the justices try! One time, Justice Breyer told Justice Ruth Ginsberg that their next case was the Jockey litigation. Justice Ginsberg couldn't find any material on the case so she went around to all the justices asking if she could see their Jockey briefs because she didn't have any. You won't find this kind of information on the SCOTUS website.

After much deliberation, the justices render a decision. The justices who win get to write the "majority opinion," otherwise known as the writ of "Told-you-so, told-you-so." The justices who didn't win get to write the "dissenting opinion." This dissenting opinion was originally called the "minority opinion" until Justices Ginsberg, Alito, Scalia, and Thomas all ended up on the same side writing the minority (losing) opinion. Imagine the headlines: "Why Do You Think

They're Called Minorities"? *The New York Times*, acting in the capacity of **amicus curiae** (see later for definition) immediately supplicated the court for a name change from 'minority' to 'dissenting'.

How does the Supreme Court operate? Do they have water coolers like other organizations?

There are about 200 subalterns running around the court doing stuff. They're not particularly important, so we will spend no time on them. What is important is that each justice is allowed to have four clerks. These clerks are chosen every 2-3 years by each justice. They had to come from the best schools, best families, best neighborhoods, and be members of secret societies that only admit themselves. The Justices interview the potential Supreme Court Clerks thoroughly and exchange secret society handshakes and then choose their favorite candidate based upon an exacting criterion: "Just how conservative are you?" This robust screening for latent signs of independence and any nagging desire to be fair, is critical to the smooth running of the Supreme Court. After all who wants a lefty, sour puss around all day??

The job of the Clerk is to help the justices think, prepare their decisions, fill in the hangman blanks and surprise their respective justice with a thoughtful, totally unanticipated birthday party at exactly the same time, in exactly the same place, with exactly the same attendees (the other Big 8) each year. Four current members of the Supreme Court were former SC Clerks. Alger Hiss was a Supreme Court Clerk but he didn't go to either the Left, the Right or the Center side - convicted of perjury he went to the dark side in the New York slammer.

Other than that, they're just like you and me. Once appointed, the clerks do all the major research for their respective justices. It is therefore important that they are well grounded in the fundamentals of the law and the Constitution so that they can either manipulate or ignore them, depending on what the circumstances dictate. However, clerks can never waiver in their opinion or especially in the face of facts. Only the Supreme Court justices can do that.

Supreme Court traditions –– who says these relics are fuddy-duddy's?

The justices greet each other each day in the court with a special handshake. This handshake was the brainchild of Chief Justice Melville Fuller way back when, when shaking hands was done with all five fingers. This handshake tradition endures to this day, presumably still with all five fingers. During this handshake tradition, the justices all put on name tags so that they can remember whom they've been talking to for the last 20 years. Occasionally this name tag stuff gets out of hand. For example: One time Justice Clarence Thomas wrote, "Hi, I'm Thurgood Marshall" on his name tag, and he and Justice Ginsberg spent the entire day talking about old times. (Not true)

Secondly, at the beginning of each session, a white quill is placed on the table of each counsel who will be arguing a case before the court that day, in case they forgot their BiC (true). This is sort of the judicial equivalent of a Holiday Inn towel. You're not supposed to take them home as a souvenir, but nobody really cares if you do.

The third tradition is that, upon nomination, each justice is given a nickname by the other justices. For example, Samuel Alito is referred to as "Sauce-Alito". I'll bet you can't guess why... It's because the other justices think his decisions resemble an Italian dish, i.e., "Alito of a-law, Alito of a-precedent, Alito of a-parmesan, and pretty soon you gotta fine landmark a-decision." We just can't spend anymore time here on the nickname stuff because our next Piece is the United Nations and we have to pick up the pace. We'll leave it at this: Chief Justice John Roberts' nickname is "Sir." This shows that there is a limit to the amount of High Jinx that will be tolerated in the High Court

Age, diversity and term limits

Two out of three is not bad! First of all, there is no question the Supreme Court has age. In fact, the average age of the current justices is 67.5 years. By comparison, the age of the first justices in 1790 was 59.8. Why is this? The answer is simple. It takes eight years longer to become out of touch today than it did in the 1700s.

Some believe that at 62 we are closing in on the geriatric Rubicon. They support their position with math (red flags for me—how about you?) They say that if the average age of the U.S. citizen is more like 30, how can these antiques be relevant? The answer, of course, is clear. They're Republicans, stupid!

Second, the Supreme Court has diversity. Matter of fact, folks on the Far Right think it may have **just a wee bit too much** diversity. Our current court has one African American, one Italian, four white guys (not capitalized) two Jews and a white Latina who are also both woman (score double points). Those of us in the Far Center believe that diversity in our highest institutions is pretty cool. However, since diversity is something that is only spoken of in polite company these days, let's just leave it at that.

Knowing important terms that Justices use daily

Before this book, only your Latin teacher really understood what the justices said after they said it. Now you can grab the latest court register and dazzle your friends with your legal knowledge—and maybe even become a paralegal like most of our U.S. Attorneys General. Here is a list of really useful phrases you will often come across:

- **Amicus Curiae:** Literally means "friend of the court." If you can find one, let us know. Even the justices aren't that wild about each other, much less someone just showing up out of nowhere wanting to be friends.
- **Courtus Interruptus:** Bathroom breaks for the justices. These usually come right after lunch and right before Alan Dershowitz's opening arguments.
- **Stare Decisis:** Pronounced *stare-ee di-SIGH-sus*, this literally translates as "This one's up to the Gods—who's up for a recess?" Not true. It actually means, "to stand by what has been decided." This phrase is often invoked at confirmation hearings (see Justice John Roberts), when nominees wish to go for the "Blow Job" (see earlier for definition). If a nominee wishes to give the "right" (correct) answer or the "left" (correct) answer, they will invoke **stare decisis**, depending on who's asking the question. For example, if some weenie senator on the left (like Chuck Shumer) asks a Supreme Court nominee what his position on abortion is, the nominee will cite Roe v. Wade as a **stare decisis** or "the court already decided this; were you at lunch"? Likewise, if some bully on the right (like Rand Paul) asks the same question, he gets the same

answer. Both senators are equally satisfied, and the hearings can go on.

- **Briefs:** Briefs are meant to be a clear, concise statement of what the lawyers intend to argue vaguely and long-windedly before the court. If a brief is five pages or longer, it must have a table of contents (true). If it is longer than five pages, it is called a "lengthy" (not true). Anything longer then a lengthy is called a Writ of Tedium and is promptly trash canned (probably true but they're not talking). Why does the court decide **not** to hear some cases? Much of it has to do with time management. As you may know, deciding the outcome of Presidential elections is not the only thing these folks do. Ruth Ginsberg is writing *The Joy of Jewish Jurisprudence*; Sammy Little Alito is an amateur chef, Clarence Thomas does standup at The Scales in downtown D.C., and so forth. When the court decides not to hear a case, it assigns Justice Ginsberg to issue a "Writ of Deaf Ear," meaning we will not hear the case and Justice Ginsberg is turning a deaf ear to the litigants. Justice Ginsberg was chosen for this because she can turn a deaf ear from both sides of her head.

- **Oral Arguments:** Oral arguments became popular with the court when it became obvious that it was impossible to become red in the face in writing. It was also difficult for lawyers to raise their voices, fists—and definitely the flag—in writing. Finally, it is almost impossible to have an argument without moving your lips (unless you're filing divorce papers). All of this weighed heavily on the hearts and minds of the justices and it meant less stuff to read.

The Center's Conclusion

Of the 112 Justices confirmed to the Supreme Court since 1789, 51 were nominated by Republican Presidents, 47 by Democratic Presidents, 14 by Federalists (whatever that is), and six by the Whigs (short for "white guys" party). Even Millard Fillmore was allowed to seat a justice, and still, after more than 200 years, the Republic rolls on! The Far Center believes the Supreme Court is a pretty good institution (even if the French like it), and the Justices have most often proved wiser than the people or process that nominated them.

CENTER PIECE 2

The United Nations

Charter: "To Meet A Lot"
Mission: "To Disagree A Lot"
Goal: "To Spend A Lot"

A brief history of this crack organization

Many knowledgeable individuals who have studied the history and accomplishments of the U.N. strongly believe that it is the biggest train wreck of a bureaucracy in the world. They have also concluded that it couldn't win the New York State lottery if it had the only ticket.

Those who dislike the U.N. are less flattering. But those of us in the Far Center are bound by our ethics to fairness. And some, like me, feel that maybe we can help. Isn't that what we're about at the Far Center? And isn't this an institution that greatly affects the United States and so should be understood by us all? The answer, of course, is "okay if you say so."

In biological terms, the Far Right believes that where some organizations are the heart and soul of a movement, the United Nations is more like the earth's appendix; that is; it serves no useful purpose, has gotten very swollen, and gets sore at its host, mostly the United States.

By contrast, the Far Left believes this is a finely tuned planetary-wide instrument that gives voice to those countries that normally wouldn't pay good money to come to New York and say sorry things about the United States when they can say these things from home.

Those of us in the Far Center believe that the problems of the U.N. go much deeper than mere mediocrity of leadership and panty-waisted courage. We believe that, like all biological problems since the beginning of time, the U.N. suffered in its infancy from limited nurturing and even less quality time with its parents. Why? Because the United Nations' mom and dad were the equally dysfunctional organization (parents) called the League of Nations.

After World War I, all the countries that liked to fight each other every 20 years (and still do) got together and said, "enough is enough". It was time for something grand sounding i.e, the Treaty of Versailles. The 44 countries that signed the treaty were called the League of Nations. The League's purpose was simple: planetary peace and security.

As an organization, its success was laudable. For 19 years (1919 to 1938), they prevented the "every 20 years" war. It's hard to argue with success isn't it? Then those darned Germans invaded Poland in 1939, starting World War II, and really screwed up what could have been, one in a row, for the League. This was the League's chance to prevent for 20 years that which only happened every 20 years, and they still messed it up. Math is a cruel mistress.

Please note: It was U.S. President Woodrow Wilson's idea to start the League of Nations. He even got the Nobel Peace Prize for it. Thanks, Woody—it was obviously a great run. Long story short, the League of Nations, clearly not in a league of its own, was not long for this world. Even politics has minimum requirements!

Therefore, being the first documented casualty of "management by objectives," the League was euthanized. But good ideas go down reluctantly. So another U.S. President, Franklin Roosevelt, started talking up a successor to the League. He was sure the idea of planetary peace and security was a good one—it was just poor execution on the part of virtually every country on earth since the beginning of time. No argument there. Where 44 countries who formed the League had failed, the 50 members of its successor would surely succeed. And voilà, **THE UNITED NATIONS WAS BORN!** On June 26, 1945, 50 countries boldly stepped up and formed the United Nations.

Anybody want to take a crack at what the goal was? Yup, "planetary peace and security." Just as a historical aside, Poland was the 51st country to join the U.N., not even one of the original 50. I mean **come on**—their getting invaded in 1939 is what started the whole thing! The least they could have done was be first in line to join up. When asked to comment, the Poles huffed and said they didn't get the memo about the end of the war until 1946.

Well that's all behind us. Now, as of June 26, 1945, we've made a fresh start, with a fresh organization and 50 fresh members with a not-so-fresh charter of "planetary peace and security". One could easily forgive the world for becoming downright giddy at this point. The great halls of peace and backslapping were full of nations proclaiming things like, "Great Scott, we're on a worldwide roll and we got a new place in downtown Manhattan. Let's go to work and show those nay-sayers we mean business!" (Reader alert—math question follows).

So...if it took 44 members of the League of Nations 19 years to avoid the 20-year war, how long would it take 50 members of the United Nations to avoid any war? Correct! Exactly four years, 364 days! North Korea invades South Korea and everybody's back at it again.

Since then it's been the French against Vietnam; India against Pakistan; Russia against all the other "Stans"; Britain against the Irish; Iran against Iraq; Israel against everybody, and the United States against ***anybody***. The list is endless. But, the Far Center does not carp; we construct. Therefore, in the last Piece of this book, we will put forward the successor to the United Nations—"The Peace Championship Series"!

Where is the United Nations located?

The U.N. is located in New York City (Manhattan). How did this happen, Mr. Center Guy? Can you tell us the history?

Many of you believe that the Indians (Shinnecock) sold Manhattan to the settlers (Dutch) for beads and buttons. If this were true, which it most certainly is not, then it would have been the first example of really crappy investment banking advice provided to anybody, much less the Indians. The truth is that on May 6, 1626, the Indians sold Manhattan to the Dutch for 60 guilders (about $30). Therefore, **this**, was the first example of really crappy investment banking advice provided to anybody! So the beads/buttons deal is a real good story, but it isn't true. If you want proof, contact the New York Historical Society, which has the 1626 letter—the only known document to mention the purchase of Manhattan by the Dutch from the Indians.

Once the Dutch took over, they hung around until about 1650. Their accomplishments while in the future Big Apple were, shall we say, "Dutch," which when translated from its Latin origins means "squat." They named the place New Amsterdam, which never caught on. And then they were caught off guard when the Brits showed up and booted them out in the "War of Something or Other." Not only that, but the brief 24 years that the Dutch owned Manhattan was hardly enough time for them to get a decent return on their 60 guilders, plus the whole episode had been embarrassing and was playing very poorly back in Amsterdam. So the Dutch made up this story about buying all of Manhattan for just beads so people wouldn't laugh at them for being poor negotiators and accuse them of wearing wooden shoes.

Why is all this stuff about Manhattan important? Because the U.N. got the best 18 acres of Manhattan for free from John D. Rockefeller Jr. (an American), and they still make funny faces at us behind our backs. To make matters worse, Rockefeller bought the land for $8.5 million and then turned around and donated it (as in for free) to the U.N. This land is cursed. First the Indians get screwed, then the Dutch get screwed, then Rockefeller screws himself, and the U.S. has been getting screwed ever since. The only thing those of us in the Far Center have to say is the following: 1) John D. Rockefeller Jr. is medical proof that intelligence skips a generation, 2) this gift of land to the U.N. is a constant reminder that "no good deed will go unpunished" (see also the Marshall Plan, Liberation of France, Kuwait, Iraq, etc.) and 3) the Indians should have held out for an IPO.

So the U.N. accepts the 18 acres and is now the U.S.'s permanent "roomy", **rent free**.

What really is the purpose of the U.N.?

Many people argue that the U.N. is not here to keep peace, but rather to do lots of other good things. If any organization does lots of good things, it's the U.N. We're just concerned that these things aren't what Woody and the original 44 countries of the League, plus Franklin and the 50 countries who founded the U.N., had in mind. So unlike this Manhattan-for-beads story, let's get to the truth.

From **The Preamble to the Charter of the United Nations**:

"We the People of the United Nations (are) determined to save succeeding generations from the scourge of war, which twice in our lifetime has brought untold sorrow to mankind..."

From **Article I, Chapter I, of The United Nations Charter:**

The purposes of the United Nations are:

1) To maintain international peace and security and to that end: to take effective and collective measures for the prevention and removal of threats to the peace."

Assuming that the Preamble and Article I, Chapter I, carry some sort of **a priori** importance, then the Far Center's going to go out on a limb here and say that some, just some, of the 109 U.N. committees and commissions might not be perfectly aligned with what this organization was originally designed to do, **and,** that some of the U.N.'s "peacekeeping" efforts have not exactly been laced with "ass-kicking" resolve.

We'll talk about U.N. finances later, but these guys spend $20 billion each year, and many folks would like to see the proverbial ball across the end zone occasionally. For $20 billion, we could elect a President every year! Anyway, the history of "can't we all just get along" hasn't been too stellar since the U.N.'s founding.

For example, at no moment in the history of this planet, even with Daylight Saving Time, has the world not been experiencing **at least** 10 separate and simultaneous wars on five continents, with a combined loss of life of 28 million (very true). Can you imagine where we'd be if these guys' charter was Planned Parenthood?

We might as well get this all off our chest right now. Do you know what else? During this same period of time, when all these wars were being waged and people were getting killed by the truckload, the U.N., or one of its organizations, was awarded 10 separate Nobel Peace Prizes! The most recent Nobel Prize was awarded in 2013 to the Organization for the Prohibition of Chemical Weapons. What an outreach program they have with Bashar Al-Assad of Syria. Hooray and hooray! In 2001 the Peace Prize was given to the former U.N. Secretary General Kofi Annan and the entire U.N. for their successful efforts in the fight against terrorism, which we all know is behind us. We're pretty sure the Marx Brothers have returned to Earth as the Nobel Nominating Committee.

Leadership and organization of the U.N.

If the U.N. has any real problem, it's that it is not able to relate to the "folks." Why is this? It's because the leaders of the U.N. — the Secretaries General — seem distant. As an example, some of U.N. Secretaries have had names like Trygve, Dag, U Thant, and Boutros-Boutros, Kofi Anan, Ban Ki Moon.

By contrast, the United States has most recently elected, for **our** Presidents, people with first names like George; Dick (just kidding); Bill, twice; and George (the second), twice. We even had a Harry, and our first President was also a George. These are names that the people can wrap their hearts around. I can't even wrap my tongue around Trygve! Our current Secretary General's whole name is Ban Ki Moon, which I keep wanting to pronounce Monkey Boon. Selecting these people, with names like these, is a gift that simply can't be coached. But I personally am having a hard time relating. This book will help all of us.

These people, with their exotic-sounding names, come from smallish countries that have few enemies and no axe to grind. Being liked at the U.N. is important—just ask the U.S. So why isn't Russia or the U.S. or Great Britain the head of the U.N.? After all, we pick up most of the tab for its expenses. The answer is: unknown.

But those of us in the Far Center believe that this is OK. If all the power of the U.N. were concentrated in the hands of the "big dogs," then what would happen? Chaos! Russia would probably invade Crimea; the U.S. would invade Iraq; China would steal all our DVD's; and North Korea would develop a nuke.

Perhaps the larger countries could learn from the smaller ones! For example, two of our Secretaries General have come from Norway and Sweden, respectively. These two countries have good-looking women, low crime rates, and very effective healthcare systems, not to mention some of the highest per-capita incomes in the world. One Secretary General came from Peru. In Peru, they have neat sightseeing, and the women wear men's hats. Another came from Egypt, where they export olives, pictures of old stones, and **hatred**. But by and large, these countries are neutral and, like Ghana, give us, well, um, **air**, which is fine.

At this point, the Far Center feels duty-bound to offer into nomination the next secretary general of the United Nations. In keeping with the theme of "planetary peace and security" and "smaller is better," we are proud to nominate... **Woody Allen**.

Why is he such a fine choice? First, Woody is a real name, and, as we have discussed previously, that's important. Second, he married his own adopted daughter, Soon Yi Previn, which means family is important to him. Third, since his wife is Asian, he obviously gets along well with more than half the world's population. And finally, he would have the best campaign motto of anybody:

Soon Yi—Soon Peace
The Woody Way

The organization of the U.N. is not quite as clear as mud. As of 2007, there were 193 U.N. members, meaning 193 nations. In 1984, there were 159 member nations. How is this possible? Is the Earth growing? No it isn't, but neither is all this "planetary peace and security" jive.

Every few years, due to religious, sectarian, or "I just don't like you" violence, some countries blow themselves up and become many separate countries. Here is a great example: Yugoslavia used to be a country. It was also one of the founding 50 members of the U.N. in 1945. In 1992 Yugoslavia blew itself up and became; 1) Bosnia Herzegovinia, 2) Croatia, 3) Slovenia, 4) Macedonia, 5) Serbia, and 6) Montenegro. At this rate the U.N. is going to need at least another 18 acres. Since we don't have any more chumps like Rockefeller around, maybe we could get Trump to be the chump and provide the necessary acreage for growth of the organization.

For some of the 193 countries that come to the U.N. headquarters in New York, it is the first time they get to wear a clean shirt. For other countries, these gatherings are pretty old hat. For example, the Europeans don't like to go because they have to bathe. The U.S. doesn't like to go because nobody likes them. But for one country, it's still a mystery. There is still one long-time member nation that still hasn't shown up at the U.N. in New York. The reason is that the Brits told them the meetings were held in New Hampshire! Presumably, this merriment will continue to the utter delight of **all** the members of the U.N., because as soon as this country discovers the ruse, the Brits will still have New Jersey and New Mexico to work with. Who says humor doesn't translate? Can you guess the country, reader? (Answer in The Sorbet).

Supporting these 193 countries, or at least the 191 that show up, are six Organs and 103 Commissions. The six Organs are the ones that really run the show and are as follows: General Assembly; Security Council; Economic and Social Council; Trusteeship Council; International Court of Justice; and Secretariat (not the racehorse).

These are called Organs because they are critical to the functioning body of the U.N. This would be like your heart, liver, bowels (?) but not the appendix. The most important of these organs (referred to as the tallest midget) is the Security Council.

The permanent members of the Security Council are China, France, Russia, Great Britain, and the United States. The only thing these countries ever had in common was that the last time "planetary peace and security" did **not** break out, they were the only countries left standing.

In addition to these permanent members, there are 10 non-permanent members of the Security Council. Nobody on the earth can explain to me why we have these members. They have no vote, no shtick, and pretty much no voice in what happens. They don't even get to sit up front. The only thing we do know is that if one of the permanent members does something nobody likes, the non-permanent members get to boo and whistle-loudly. These boo's and whistles are translated from their native tongue into English, so the U.S. doesn't miss anything. The translation is usually much like the comments you might hear in the Oakland Raiders' nickel seats when the visiting team scores. Matter of fact, when the colleagues at the U.N. meet they are either giving each other the finger **under** the table or grand-fucking each other **over** the table.

The U.N. has many other councils/commissions that seem to be, at best, troubling. For example, the Council for Outer Space Affairs meets in Vienna, Austria. The only thing close to Outer Space that Austria ever gave the world was Arnold "The Über Güber" Swarzenegger.

This council also has deliberations on "Space Law" (true). What could Space Law be about? Why would anyone admit to knowing about it or being a part of it? If a U.S. spaceship makes an illegal right turn into some Russian piece of flying junk, do we dispatch a space cadet from Earth to measure spatial skid marks?

This council also proudly points out that "developing countries" (definition: dirt poor) use the council to help predict weather, since most developing countries don't have their own weatherman on at 10 p.m. each night. I don't think weather reports to people who are starving is the highest good the U.N. could conceive. Here's some low-tech advice, from me, at an even lower cost—without the help of a space councilor's satellite: "Bulletin to all Saharan and sub-Saharan countries. It's going to be hot, dry, and shitty tomorrow—and for the next 364 days after that."

How about the International Seabed Authority? Who knows!? Just assume the Seabed Authority has about as much impact as the Outer Space guys, except underwater.

Finally, the United Nations has a "Convention to Combat Desertification," which is held in Bonn, Germany. Bonn, Germany, is approximately 2,000 miles north of the nearest desert. This makes perfect sense to the U.N.-ites, but I think something closer to Riyadh, Saudi Arabia, might just be the ticket. Let's move on to something even more depressing.

Financing the U.N.

At long last! The Far Left, the Far Right and the Far Center are in perfect agreement: everybody dislikes how the U.N. is financed. All 193 participating countries are obliged to make contributions to the U.N.'s $20 billion annual budget. None of these countries feel properly represented or appreciated. The way the Far Center looks at it is this: The major committees of the United Nations, the six we spoke of earlier, are called the U.N. Organs. All 193 countries are Donors. Therefore each country should be proud to be an Organ Donor.

Each country is supposed to donate its fair share of the $20 billion based on its respective GDP. GDP stands for gross domestic product and kind of means, "did I make anything last year and sell it, or did I just sneak across the border at Nogales?"

So, rich countries pay more and poor ones pay less. This is the only fair thing about the U.N. and, of course, everybody hates it.

Nobody generally pays on time, except The Holy See (true). The U.S., when it does pay, which is always late, pays the most. Some hellhole in Africa probably pays the least, and that is as it should be.

The only thing that all members can generally agree on is that in 2004, The Netherlands paid the fifth most of any country into the U.N. budget. Who said there isn't a God? These bastards started the whole thing by screwing over the Indians, so they can jolly well pay the piper now.

The Centers' Conclusion

At the end of the day, the Far Center believes that the only thing worse than having a United Nations is not having a United Nations. The U.N. does lots of good and seldom any harm, and that's more than you can say for at least 90 percent of its member countries. The fact that little twits like Robert Mugabe of Zimbabwe, global warming, terrorism, and patently stupid foreign policy statements by Joe Biden are still with us doesn't mean anything, other than there is still work to do.

The Far Center would like to mention two people who, during the Iraq War debate, underscored the need to have a U.N. in order to provide neutral ground for countries to disagree vehemently and peacefully: former U.S. Secretary of State Colin Powell was our representative during this period. To Powell goes the Purple Heart for having been shot in the foot by Don Rumsfeld and having fallen on his sword for his country.

CENTER PIECE 3

The Electoral College

Motto: "Your Vote Doesn't Count".

History of the Electoral College

As we all know, not everyone in a college is smart; but it's a good bet that at least two or three people at each college are. In some schools, these people can number in the tens. Sometimes, like at Harvard, almost everyone is smart because they all get "A"s all the time. That's what differentiates the Electoral College from all other colleges. Nobody in the Electoral College is too bright, their grades aren't very good, and their parents still don't take their car away. How can this be? Well, it's because it's a college for politicians. Enough said! To understand the Electoral College, you must first understand why we have it, where it came from, and if there is any cure for it. The answers to those three questions are: 1) because, 2) the Constitution, and 3) no.

The Framers of the Constitution, otherwise known as the signers of the Declaration of Independence, had a lot on their plate back in the late 1700s. First they wrote the Declaration of Independence, then the British came over to America and said, "Not so fast." Then we all fought each other for eleven years. We won; they lost.

So what happened after that? I'm glad you asked. A Declaration of Independence is no good without a Constitution, because a Constitution is supposed to "constitute" what you were "declaring" in your declaration. You must have both documents to start your own country. This is why Yugoslavia, as we so vividly learned in the last Piece on the United Nations, blew themselves up into six different countries. **They didn't "declare" and they didn't "constitute"**. So what happened? Instead of having a neat name like "America," Yugoslavia became several different countries with unattractive names like Herzegovina and Croatia and Montenegro, among others.

This is a poor outcome. For example, how do you develop a tourist trade if people don't even know where you are and travel agents can't spell your name and so don't know how to look you up? In Montenegro, the government immediately recognized this problem and decided to run a contest among the citizens to see who could come up with the best slogan to introduce the country to the world. So far they have two finalists: 1) We're from Montenegro and You Are Ugly and 2) "Welcome to Montenegro, would you like to see my Yugo?" Those of us in the Far Center believe the time would be better spent developing a Constitution!

The Framers and Founders—and virtually everyone else in our country—knew you could run into a lot of problems starting your own country (like Montenegro did). So they made sure they had a good declaration and a good constitution. This involved a lot of "pursuits" and "manifests," many "destinies," lots of "rights," and no "wrongs." In the process of all of this, some goof (who will be identified later) decided that nobody had figured out how you get a President. After all, they didn't have Presidents in England; they had kings and queens. The way you got these kings and queens was through years of meticulous and purposeful inbreeding. Nobody was **ever** elected.

Stop right there, Mr. Far Center guy. Would you please come to the point about the Electoral College?

I am coming to the point. The Electoral College sprang from the loins of the Constitution because we needed a fair and uniform way to elect the president of our new country. And in the future, don't rush me again!

If I may continue... Article 2, Section 1 of the Constitution of the United States was written to give us the least screwed up way to elect a President. And therefore, **THE ELECTORAL**

COLLEGE WAS BORN! But many of you may ask the Far Center, "Why didn't we just decide to vote on the guy who was running for office? You know, the 'one-man-one-vote' deal"? The answer is clear and sensible—if you are a politician **and** live on the East Coast. The Framers were afraid (and this is true) that if you let a bunch of backwoods yahoos (commonly referred to as "the voter") elect a President by popular vote, then just think what a mess of it they might make. The voter might easily be duped by empty promises and good haircuts. And if that were not enough, extravagant traveling puppet shows would show up at every town hall with grave concern on their little puppet faces, to ask in their little fake voices, for your vote. By contrast, you couldn't let the Congress elect a President, because the voting official might easily be duped by empty promises and good haircuts—wait, didn't I just say this?

So a compromise was reached. You may have heard the word "compromise" used often when referring to anything related to politics. Compromise means "agreement" in Congress-speak. It is defined as follows: "Wherever there are two perfectly good alternatives to any problem, Congress will always come up with a mediocre third."

At this point in our history, we needed one of those "compromises," So up steps fellow Framer Mr. James Wilson Esq., who was selected to write the rules of the Electoral College. Those who hate the Electoral College have said that Wilson wasn't one of the real signers of the Declaration and was nothing more than an **alternate**, who never would have gotten to sign the Declaration at all if Wallace Figmore from Rhode Island hadn't called in sick that day (not true). Those of us in the Center do not chase ugly rumors. All we know for sure is that James Wilson attended a lot of colleges but never graduated from any of them (true). So he jumped on the chance to found his own college and shove it up everybody's nose.

How does the Electoral College work?

Poorly, unless you're a big believer in chance––then the answer is... **perfectly**! America takes pride in the institutions that support its republic. We are self-congratulatory about how these institutions evolve in order to adapt to changing times and needs. For example, we learned earlier, in the piece on the Supreme Court, that the court evolved over 200 years from "finger-giving" to "finger pointing" and now to hardy handshakes with all five fingers. The United Nations is also evolving (slowly). I am afraid to say that the Electoral College may be an exception to its institutional counterparts.

As you have probably gathered by now, the Electoral College isn't really a college at all. If it were, I would have gone there, because I could have gotten in and I could have gotten out (meaning I could have graduated). It's also not located anywhere, but if it were, it would be in California. This will be discussed later, under the general heading of "I'm beginning to get concerned." So the Electoral College is basically nothing, located nowhere, whose students only attend through correspondence. However, it is one thing: it is the powerful system through which we elect our nation's Presidents.

In 1788, it was decided that each state would be given "Electoral" votes equal to the number of senators and representatives each state had. Today each state is given Electoral votes equal to the number of senators and representatives each state has. Those two previous sentences may sound redundant to you, you uniformed backwoods yahoo voter. But to those of us who really understand stuff, this is just further proof of the Framers' wisdom and the Constitution's durability. Or said another way, "The more things change the less the Electoral College does!" Anyway, once each state had collected all its' votes, the results were mailed to, and counted in, Washington. The results were then verified by an accounting firm—like Arthur Andersen—that had impeccable credentials?? (Out of business)

Our first Presidential election was held in 1788, when George Washington was running largely unopposed. There were only nine states, with a total of 69 Electoral votes. George sweeps—the math was easy—everybody thinks the system is just fine. And the reason it was just fine was that **there was no popular vote being counted!** But in the Presidential election of 1874 someone decided that we were going to start counting the popular vote (you know, the backwoods yahoos), and *voilà* (French for "Oh shit!"), something didn't add up. John Adams was running against Andrew Jackson for President. First Jackson gets **more** popular votes than Adams. Then Jackson gets more Electoral votes than Adams. Guess who won—Adams, of course. How is this possible? Because those of us in the Far Center blame George W. Bush.

If this was just a one-time fluke, we would all understand and that would be that. But it keeps happening. In 1888, Benjamin Harrison loses the popular vote to Grover Cleveland but wins the Electoral vote—so, *voilà, déjà vu* (French for, "Oh shit, not again!"), Harrison wins. Then in 2000, Al Gore gets more popular votes than George Bush, but Bush wins. It's bound to happen again. And every time it does happen, people become very red-in-the-face and say they are going to leave the U.S. permanently and move to Harvard University.

So why don't we fix the problem and get rid the Electoral College? Because the Electoral College is part of the Constitution, and in order to change the Constitution you have to have an Amendment and that takes three-fourths of each of the states legislatures to agree to the change. Has it ever been tried? No. Will it ever be tried? No. Why? Because you couldn't get three-fourths of the states to agree on which side of the Earth the sun is coming up tomorrow, much less a Constitutional Amendment.

In the last 200 years, the U.S. has grown from nine states with 69 Electoral votes to 50 states with 538 Electoral votes. In order to win the presidency today (math alert) one must get 270 Electoral votes (one more than half of the 538). Well, let's do the math! On second thought, let's not.

The Electoral College Calculator

The only thing worse than doing the wrong thing, is doing the wrong thing real well!! That about sums it up. Nobody likes the Electoral College but nobody has a better idea, so we just keep perfecting what we've got. That is to say, we can at least add to the 270 votes and still ignore the popular vote.

There has been one minor change. Nebraska and Maine allow their Electoral votes to be split, based roughly on their states' popular vote. The only problem is that between them they only have nine Electoral votes, so nobody cares.

Here's a fun exercise for readers. Who has the most Electoral votes? Alaska plus Delaware plus Hawaii plus Montana plus New Hampshire plus North Dakota plus South Dakota plus Rhode Island with 6.3 million combined population—**or**, Florida, with 18.1 million in population? Congratulations, you are absolutely correct. Neither! They both have 27 Electoral votes. Therefore the 18.1 million people in Florida have no more Electoral clout than the 6.3 million people in the eight states largely populated by animals.

If you really like the Electoral College, then the news just keeps getting better. Why? Because over the last five years, the average growth rate of the states with the 6.3 million population mentioned above was over 5 percent. By contrast, Florida's growth rate over the same period was over 13 percent. Apparently, the Electoral College calculator needs new batteries!

The Far Right believes that in order to correct this failing grade in math, the U.S. should immediately invade Cuba, make it part of Miami, which would be seamless, and assign Florida 10 more Electoral votes. The Far Left believes we should give Florida to Cuba, which would also be seamless, and the problem would go away.

Every time we add a state, we add new Electoral votes. As mentioned before, there are now 538 Electoral votes (435 for each member of the House of Representatives, 100 for each member of the U.S. Senate, and three for the District of Columbia, which represents the President, Vice President, and the Washington Redskins). Unless we invade Cuba, the 538 Electoral votes is not going to change. So how **do** we correct the situation described above?

Every ten years the U.S. conducts what is known as the Census. This is where poor mooks, hired by the government, go to every door in the United States and ask how many people live there. Then they add it all up, and if it looks like one state grew a lot and another didn't, then the 538 Electoral votes are reapportioned. Reapportionment is taking Electoral votes from one state and giving them to another. Think of the importance of this. If you're from Massachusetts and hate George Bush and all the other Bushes—and the state of Texas because of them—then you hope the Massachusetts population grows and the Texas population decreases so that in the next election Massachusetts will have more Electoral votes and John Kerry can lose by a smaller margin.

As you can readily imagine, this Census is serious business to politicians, because it is the first chance for them to affect an election legally. Since politicians are not too experienced at this, they have clandestinely created what we in the Far Center believe are called "block parties." How does a block party work, and is it a threat to our national security?

During the Census, the census taker (mook) goes, for example, to House A. He counts the people there and then goes on to House B. What he doesn't know is that all the people from House A have now run across their backyard into House B, put on their Groucho Marx fake faces, and act like they live in House B. The census taker counts them all and goes on from house to house. This sort of thing keeps up until everybody (about 200) are in the last house on the block, all looking like close relatives of Groucho Marx. Regrettably, intelligence from the Far Center, has indicated that the people most likely to engage in this deception are the Far Right in Texas. When this was discovered, the people on the Far Left immediately started their own block party on the Harvard University campus. The only problem was that instead of **Groucho** Marx masks they all put on **Karl** Marx masks and were quickly discovered.

Can a moron be elected President by mistake?

NO! We do that every four years, **ON PURPOSE!**

Who are these Electors?? I've never met one!

You are in good company. Nobody else has ever met an elector, either. The whole concept of an elector began in the Roman Empire in 962 A.D., when certain people who were well connected, got to decide who would be the next emperor. These well-connected people were grouped into what the Romans called a "collegium," from which we get the Electoral College. Collegium is defined as: "We all get along because we all think alike." Thinking alike was important when selecting an emperor, because being on an emperor's bad list had its downside. For example, if the final Electoral count was Nero: 23, Flavius: 1, and you were the **one**, then the chances of you ending up taking a dirt nap in Tuscany were pretty high.

Just for your information, there are other "colleges" in our world. There is the College of Cardinals in Rome. These folks get to select the Pope, and when they do select a Pope, they make "white smoke" in the Vatican. Our Electoral College gets to select the U.S. President, and when they select a President, they make water in their pants.

Like in Roman times, our electors are well-connected people who support the "right" emperor. The name "elector" comes from the Latin, meaning *"particus hackus"* or "I promise to think alike."

Anyway, let's wrap up with this. When you vote you don't really vote for the President; you vote for his electors. (Reader, prepare for a long sentence). Since you never got to vote for an elector in the first place, because you were never invited to the state convention where electors are chosen in the second place, and if you are not connected, much less well-connected in the third place, then the chance of your vote counting the way you thought it would is next to absolute zero in the fourth place.

What if 'this' keeps going on like 'this'?

Earlier I pointed out to you that **"I'm beginning to become concerned."** This is the section where we report on that concern, as expressed by the Far Right. When the Electoral College was conceived in 1788, it had 69 Electoral votes; then it increased to 138 in 1796 and then 352 in 1872 and so on. As states were added, we added Electoral votes. No big deal. **Except for one little thing**. In 1849, California had zero Electoral votes, and today it has 55. California has, by far, more Electoral votes today than any state, and more than 10 percent of the total Electoral vote. In addition, and please do not overlook this, the former governor of California **spoke with an accent** and was born, **in the foreign country of Austria!** If that weren't enough, need I remind you that California has the biggest immigration problem on the planet Earth! Well the Far Right has gone into hyper-speed and developed what they call "Action Armageddon." The Far Right believes that, left unchecked, by the year 2020 we will elect somebody named Jorge Benito from Chihuahua, Mexico, who speaks with an even bigger accent, because of a poor Electoral system and a por*ous* border.

Center Reader Alert––Center Reader Alert: What follows are the strategies and sentiments of the Far Right, and the Far Right only:

In order to properly address the Immigration Problem and the Electoral Problem California has caused, the following will be put to popular vote to wit and therefore: First, the Electoral Problem will be solved with the swift use of the Yugoslavia Sanction. If you recall, in both this Piece, and in the United Nations Piece, we discussed that Yugoslavia decided to just blow themselves up because things didn't look good for restructure without "declares" and "constitutes." Case closed—blow up the Electoral College! Even the burnt pieces that land in Massachusetts will be better than what we had before.

The Center's Conclusion

The Center is conflicted. There is something appealing about the Yugoslavia Sanction when you think that the Electoral College gave us U.S. President Millard Fillmore. On the other hand, keeping this system around into the 2016 Presidential election could, due to the sheer number of Presidential candidates, throw the election into a mathematical mess that could take until 2020 to sort out. And then the new moron would only be around for two years. Decision: Keep it as it is until somebody comes up with a better idea like one hand of five-card-draw poker.

CENTER PIECE 4

Vice Presidents, First Ladies and Second Place

Motto: Is There Any Difference?

Vice Presidents
"Where The Gene Pool Is Always Out Of Water."

Fill in any face you want, they're all the same.

We're first going to spend a few pages on Vice Presidents, which is a few pages more than they warrant. Then we will move smartly to a discussion of first ladies. However, an interesting historical parallel exists between Vice Presidents and first ladies, which the reader will be well served to know. To wit:

The National First Ladies Library seems to be dedicated almost solely to informing the public about which china each First Lady preferred and why, versus the indisputable contribution that each has made, somewhere, to something. That first ladies would principally be remembered for their selection of china, is decidedly un P.C. and is a slap in the face to all first ladies with the possible exception of Eleanor Roosevelt, who appeared to have been slapped around enough. Everybody knows that first ladies can do other things—like nit-pick.

For example, Florence Harding (President Warren Harding's wife) was quoted as saying, "I know what's best for the President. I put him in the White House. He does well when he listens to me, and poorly when he does not." (true). Whatever china she picked, the smart money says some of it ended up over Warren's head until he got his mind right.

To be fair, first ladies also plant trees in ghettos and support health care systems that don't pass the giggle test.

Anyway, here's the historical tidbit. All first ladies get to choose their own china. What isn't known is that Henry A. Wallace, our 33rd Vice President under Franklin Roosevelt, also got to choose his own china. Problem is, he chose poorly. He strongly advised President Roosevelt that the United States' international policy toward our friends in the East should be centered on Taiwan, China, instead of Mainland, China.

As a result, we now we have 23 **million** people who love us in Taiwan, China, and 1.3 **billion** who hate us in Mainland, China. I don't know about you, but I wouldn't want Henry Wallace as **my** math teacher. (We were unable to verify this story, but given the way government works, in general, it seems plausible).

Roosevelt was not pleased! Wallace was canned and retired to Iowa to write his memoirs, *Place Settings of the Rich and Famous*, and was never heard from again. The only thing Wallace doesn't know is that because of his foreign policy disaster he is forever referred to as "The biggest Chink in Roosevelt's armor." He was replaced with Harry S. Truman, who spent the next 82 days waiting for Roosevelt to die. Harry was particularly well qualified for the job because he didn't even know that we had developed the atom bomb until Roosevelt died. (Incredible as it may seem––this is absolutely true.)

OK, throw cold water on your face and let's see if we can't get through the next section on Vice Presidents.

The office of Vice President is considered so critical to the smooth operation of the United States that fully 14 of our 43 Presidents (33 percent) never bothered to even have a V.P. during certain portions of their Presidential tenure. The Presidential record holder is James Madison who was Prez. from 1809 to 1817. He went without a Vice President for four of his eight years, and when he finally chose one, he took Elbridge Gerry! Please put this name with United Nations luminaries like Ban Ki, Kofi and U (as in U Thant) for the "You Can't Make Up a Name Like That" award.

Anyway, more factual stuff to follow. First, Elbridge was smart enough to recognize a dead-end job, so in less than a year he died. Second, the lost art of how to rig an election by changing the way voting districts are drawn up within each state—you guessed it, Gerrymandering—comes from dear old Elbridge. Proving once again, as with Henry Wallace, that these guys can do maximum damage in a limited time frame.

How do people get a job like Vice President of the United States?

Mostly by coming in second! In our early Presidential elections, whoever came in second ended up as the V.P. When George Washington ran against John Adams for President, George got more Electoral votes than John, so George won AND John became V.P. Pretty clean system and there was no shame in being V.P. But this was mostly because there was only one political party.

When the two-party system arrived with the election of 1796, the two guys running against each other (Adams and Jefferson) were from different parties. Adams won, and all hell broke loose because Jefferson became the V.P. and didn't like Adams all that much, and vice-versa. So now we have the 12th Amendment to the Constitution that makes the Electoral College vote for a President **and** a Vice President.

Those of us in the Far Center believe that the 12th Amendment should be abolished and that we go back to the old system! Why? Because this could be the first chance for the U.S. to have a Presidential election where nobody wins and we end up with **two** Vice Presidents. The possibilities for improvement to our current system are limitless.

First, the reputation of the office of Vice President would be greatly enhanced, and people like former Vice President John Nance Garner would no longer say things like, "The office of Vice President is not worth a pitcher of warm piss" (true).

Second, for the first time in our history, there would be a Vice Presidential Library. Just think—two ghastly $10 million Vice Presidential Libraries without one book between them, versus one ghastly $20 million Presidential Library without a book. Talk about no longer being a "pitcher of warm piss"!

Third, we would have two "second ladies" instead of just one old battleaxe First Lady! Just think again, two sets of china and twice as many trees in the ghetto.

For the time being, the 12th Amendment stands, and the guy nominated by his party for President gets to pick his own Vice President. This is a weighty decision, not unlike the selection of wallpaper for the attic. Future Presidents pick Veeps they believe can help them.

In reality, Richard Nixon was right when he said in 1968, "Vice Presidents can't help you, they can only hurt you." Very prophetic indeed, coming from the man who gave us Spiro Agnew!

When the discussion of a running mate takes place among a future President's advisers, the discussion usually centers around the candidate's weak points and then, secondly, the candidate's lack of strong points. In political circles, this is referred to as the "nada round" or "nada nod" for short.

Once the nod is given and the advisors have assured themselves that the candidate has no demonstrable attributes, a test is administered, by trained medical professionals, which measures SMS output. SMS stands for "**Still Mind Syndrome**," and has consistently been an accurate indicator of just how flaccid a Vice President's mind must be. The final process in the selection is one hand of five-card stud—deuces and one-eyed jacks wild.

All told, this selection process can last well into the night. For instance, Ronald Reagan selected George H.W. Bush as his Vice President at 3 a.m. in a Detroit hotel room. The mind wonders! If Reagan had gone to bed at 11 p.m., would we still have a father-and-son presidency that has invaded every country in the world that looks like a poorly raked sand trap?

Once all this is done, the Vice Presidential candidate is approached and admonished that, for the good of the nation, for the good of the world, and for the good of all future generations, he must drop everything and become Vice President. The President then announces at the party convention that he has chosen Dan Quayle as his Vice Presidential running mate!

Stop right there, Mr. Center guy, haven't we had other people than Dan Quayle as Vice President? Answer: No. Every Vice President since Dan Quayle has, in point of fact, been Dan Quayle dressed differently and with a fake nose.

Is there anything else I should know about the Vice President?

Not really. He lives in the National Observatory where he can be closely watched (ergo the name National Observatory). He is Chairman of the board at NASA and head honcho at the Smithsonian.

Everything the Vice President does is ceremonial (worthless). He goes to royal weddings; occasionally some goobers' funeral in hell, and gets to read *The New York Times* after the President has finished with it.

In the rare event that he goes to the office (referred to as the floor of the United States Senate), he gets a big chair, is called the President of the Senate, and can only vote "yes."

Hold it. Can you explain that last statement? Yes. The Constitution says the President of the Senate has only one vote and he can't use it unless there is a tie vote. However, in the Senate, a tie vote is considered a no vote.

Stay with me on this. So if the Vice President (President of the Senate) voted no again it would be a "no-no," because the vote was already considered a "no." So if there is a tie he can only vote "yes" in order to break the tie. And you thought your government was screwed up! By the way, this is all true.

The President of the United States is required to take an oath of office upon his inauguration. The oath is the standard stuff about being over 21 years old and promising to defend something he never read (the Constitution).

However, the Vice President does **not** take an oath of office (true). What **is** administered however, is the Oaf of Office. The Oaf is given in the hallway just outside of the Oval Office with all the gravitas of a New Orleans funeral. The Oaf of Office is administered by the party's "whip" (I don't know what it means either) and goes like this:

"I (state your name), do solemnly swear (affirm) that I will perform the duties of my office daily, except weekends, when I'm off. If elected on the Republican ticket, I promise to support the President's plan to delete wasteful government programs which give costly, useless, aid to: **D**iverse, **R**acial and **E**thnic **G**roups or (**DREG**'s). Instead, I will support the government's plan to give these po' folks less and less, with more and more money until I'm providing them nothing with everything. So help me, honest injun."

"If elected on the Democratic ticket, I promise to support the President's plan to provide: **G**reater **R**ewards **U**nder **N**ew **T**axation or (**GRUNT**) to penalize all the mean-spirited wage earners who make the running of this country possible and give all those tax revenues to the **DREG**'s. So help me, honest injun."

The Centers' Conclusion

As mentioned before, abolish the 12th Amendment. If you can have this much fun with one Vice President, think what we could do with two.

First Ladies

First Ladies: *"I am naturally the most unambitious of women, and life in the white house has no attractions for me".*
—*Ellen Louise Wilson,*
wife of President Woodrow Wilson.

The First Lady, to be called First Lady, was Dolly Madison in 1849. Unfortunately it was at her funeral, so she didn't get to enjoy it. Speaking of which, she also got a cupcake named after her and she didn't get to enjoy that either. Being ahead of your time as a First Lady apparently doesn't pay off.

However, because of Dolly, and unlike intelligence, the name, **First Lady**, caught on quickly in Washington, D.C., and has been in use ever since.

First ladies, as we pointed out earlier, design china for the White House and do other remarkably forgettable stuff. Lady Bird Johnson decided that we as a nation, struggling with a huge misunderstanding in Viet Nam brought on by the careless actions of a Vice President, needed a highway beautification project! There's nothing like a deciduous here and there to lift a fella's spirits.

So she planted a gazillion trees along the interstates. Her reward? Years later Charles Kuralt was quoted as saying, "Thanks to the interstate highway system, it is now possible to travel from coast to coast without seeing anything." Irrespective, those of us in the Center love trees.

By international standards, the United States, up to this point, has had some fairly tame first ladies. By contrast, check out Imelda Marcos. She was the First Lady of the Philippines. But as soon as her husband Ferdinand died, she decided that she was perfectly qualified to be President, especially since all of her opponents proved their unreliability by shooting themselves in the back of the head. "Come on! We need leadership. Somebody's got to step up!" So Filipinos enjoyed a seamless transition. Imelda took over and immediately started kicking some serious ass with all those new shoes.

And what about Eva Peron of Argentina? They even wrote a song about her when she died. It was something about "Don't cry for me, Argentina." Are you kidding me? What's to cry for? She was rich as hell. Do you think with all that money she was satisfied with sashaying around the Blue Room with a Swifter. No sir. She took over and made hubby Juan look like Juan the Wimp.

But as mean as Eva and Imelda were, the people just loved them. Could this happen to us? You're right, Center reader, I smell something, too!

It is entirely possible that the United States of America may elect, as President of the United States (POTUS), a former First Lady of the United States (FLOTUS), and the First Person would be termed a SCRTUM or Senior Cad Resigned to an Unhappy Marriage.

Yes. We believe Hillary will break out of the China syndrome under which previous First Ladies have labored and become Imelda/Eva incarnate.

Raise your voices now in that near spiritual by Herman and The Hermits as they sing a tune about 'Enry the Eighth.

If you're Liberal move your hips back and forth in Miley Cyrus enthusiasm; if you're Conservative give it your best finger wave with both hands; as usual if you're an Independent, just stand around with your thumb in your rear until somebody tells you how to vote:

*"I'm Hillary The Great I **Y'AM***
*Hillary The Great, I **Y'AM** I **Y'AM** I got*
married to the Goober next door
*Now **HEEE** wants to be The First Lady, **AND MORE***
*We tell the folks that you can get **'Two for One'***
*But the Republicans hope **I'mmm One and Done***
*I'm Hillary the Great I **Y'AM**, I **Y'AM***
*Hillary the great I **Y'AM***

The Centers' Conclusion

We're pretty much on First Lady Laura Bush's page. When asked what she thought the role of the First Lady should be, she replied: "Whatever the First Lady wants it to be."

The Literary Sorbet

Undeniably, the French's finest contribution to civilized society has been the 'Sorbet". The Sorbet roughly translates into that culinary opportunity to pause over a cool, light dish between the already consumed appetizers and the yet to come, heavier, sauce laden, under-cooked, over-priced

Paris meal, served by what must be the most obnoxious, ill-tempered lout on the face of the Earth.

What follows, accordingly, is the Literary Sorbet. Your chance reader, to pause and reflect on your learning's thus far and to be challenged by other questions which will cause you to eagerly devour the next four Center Pieces of this extraordinary tome.

To wit: Using the end of the crayons without the teeth marks cursor, circle the answer below which you believe is more kind-a correct than the others.

Paul Revere was quoted in the Boston Globe as having said:
- "The end is near"
- "Whatever you do, don't invent a Federal Reserve System"
- "The British are coming"
- None of the above

President George W. Bush is famous for having said:
- "Speak unintelligibly and carry a big V.P."
- "Nuclar holocaused is a bad thing"
- "I graduated from The Electoral College in the top 53.25% of the Class.
- Take your pick

Hollywood types would rather:
- Adopt babies from Darfur because they think it is closer than Atlanta, Georgia
- Have beliefs that are more deeply held than Hillary's beliefs
- Learned their 'PolySci' from the Food Channel
- If you care, return this book and get your money back

In the early 1960's, the FBI:
- Invented topless radio to distract our enemies
- Secretly mandated that all words defined in Webster's Dictionary must begin with, "of or pertaining to", for reasons unknown.
- Invented the CIA, so the FBI wouldn't be blamed for everything
- I don't know either! But if I did, I couldn't tell you.

The motto of the IRS is:
- "You lean on us––We gonna lien on you"!
- Taxation without representation! What else is new?
- "Semper up yours" (Latin alert, reader)
- Anyone of the above works for me.

The two protagonists (French for 'people') in the Roe v. Wade Supreme Court ruling in 1973 were:
- Marcie Roe and Adam Wade who challenged the prohibition of interracial marriage in Kentucky, on the basis that it was less destructive than intercousinal marriage in Arkansas.
- The Second Amendament right to bear fish eggs in public restaurants.
- Norma L. McCorvey and Henry Wade who are both credited with torturing the U.S. legal system.
- One of the above.

The 'White House Plumbers' were:
- The original name of Led Zeppelin
- Could stop a leak better than that goofy looking Dutch kid with his finger in a dike.
- Crack leak fixers in the Nixon administration
- Definitely, absolutely no kidding, one of the above.

Is it true that one country, which is a member of the United Nations, has never shown up for a U.N. meeting because the British told them the meetings were held in New Mexico, instead of New York?

- No, of course not! The Brits told them the meetings were held in **New Hampshire**. Do your home-work next time, (Center Piece 2).

What is the only difference between Vice Presidents, First Ladies and Largely Useless?

- Largely Useless, is not a political position.
- Zip, Nada, Nichts, Klum, Betsuni. Is that clear?
- The ceremonial post held by a U.S. official who has to go to some African goober's funeral in some awful hell-hole.
- You can't go wrong on any of the above.

Who said "If you like your Doctor, I want to know his name."

- The NSA
- All of the above

Who said "The most immediate danger to the United States is climate change."

- ISIS
- Al Qaeda
- ISIL
- Putin
- Obama
- One of the above

CENTER PIECE 5

Political Commentary Where Quality Is Job Eleven

Motto: "We are the three asymptotes of political thought".

The "Self-Appointed," The "Self-Anointed," and The "Self-Absorbed"

Small math alert to follow: "Asymptote" is a geometric term for something that never really gets to where it's going. Imagine you are walking across a 100-foot bridge, and each time you go half the distance you stop. Then you go halfway again, and half again. If you keep going half the distance to the end of the bridge, you will keep getting closer and closer, but you will never get to the end. We believe the term "asymptote" perfectly describes political commentary today. It never gets done; it never gets to where it's going, and it never changes.

1) The Self-Appointed 2) The Self-Anointed 3) The Self-Absorbed

The beginnings of getting it wrong

The first known example of political commentary comes to us on the night of April 18, 1775, when Paul Revere set off from Boston for a late night soiree (French for, beer run) to Concord, Massachusetts. His purpose, as you may recall, was to warn anyone who was still awake at that hour that "the British are coming." Those of us in the Far Center believe this was the beginning of political commentary, because what Paul was purported to have said was both, wrong and loud.

It was wrong because he didn't say, "the British are coming" (to be explained in due time). It was loud because Paul was mad at the Continental Congress for only giving him a four-word part in what was otherwise one of the biggest gigs in history, and he figured that if that's all the lines he would get, he was going to ride around screaming them at the top of his lungs in order to get attention. This concept of "volume beats veracity any day" has continued in political commentary for the last 200 years.

"Excuse me Mr. Center guy, but I don't like where you're leading us here"!

Mrs. Muriel Welborn, my third-grade history teacher, taught us that Paul Revere said, "the British are coming." In addition, we know the Russians—and many other countries— weren't coming, because they didn't hate us yet. So would you please explain your Communist, historical revisionist self, so that people on the Far Left can grieve and begin to heal? Of course, we are only so happy to set the record straight! To wit:

Do you remember in the Piece on the United Nations, where the Far Center took history to task and debunked all this stuff about the Indians selling Manhattan to the Dutch for beads and buttons and stuff when they really sold out for 60 guilders (about 60 guilders worth of beads and buttons in today's market)? Well, we're at it again. This time, it's the British who need a little "outing."

First, all the settlers in New England at the time of Paul Revere's ride considered themselves to be British. This is because they had only been in America a short time and still enjoyed the company of warm beer and cold women, just as if they were back in jolly-ole-England.

So, since everyone in America was really still British, what moron would ride around in the middle of the night and scream, "we're all here again, we're all here again," which is the same thing as saying, "the British are coming"? In point of fact, Paul more than likely said, "the regulars are coming" or "the redcoats are coming." (This is very true.)

Why make such a big deal out of this? Here's why! Thanks to poorly researched political commentary about what Paul Revere really said, by the predecessor of The Boston Globe (whatever that was), every damn textbook in America has to be changed now; and this will cost a lot of money; and that money could have been spent on the wars in the Middle East; and we're going to lose in the Middle East because of this.

Secondly (and we realize this is a hurtful thing to say to the Far Right), some of the early, courageous, dedicated settlers who escaped British taxation and beer without fermentation, in order to establish the home of the free and brave, "were playing both ends against the middle." **Gasp and re-gasp!** Just what in the name of Nob Hill was going on? Once again, we'll tell you what!

Many of the American settlers at this early time in our history, weren't really sure this revolution stuff had legs.

So, in case the Brits won the war, these traitors wanted to be able to say, "What's wrong with a little taxation without representation? How else are we going to get universal health care?" This would surely make the "redcoats" think they were still loyal citizens of the British Empire and still loved crappy beer.

So if Paul went riding around saying at the top of his voice that the bad guys were coming, then that would tip off these traitorous Americans who would warn the invaders that the beer was better in America and that everybody was holed up in Lexington. (This is true, too.)

Let's wrap up. Why does this have anything to do with political commentary? Because, 1) some reporter, for some newspaper, had to have written that Paul Revere said, "the British are coming" and 2) that same reporter, only had four words to get correct and 3) that reporter could only get three of those four words correct and 4) we believe it was the Boston Globe, and 5) the Boston Globe never admitted to it and 6) the Globe just kept running it on the front page like they were doing a "Dan Rather."

Historical sidebar: The Far Left leaked sensitive information to Dan Rather that the world was flat, Rather immediately said, "This source is unimpeachable, I go to their dinner parties all the time, let's run with the story at the top of the 6:00 o'clock news".

Here are some more things that are going to hurt very badly, but we must get them out in the open. Paul never made it to Concord. He was arrested someplace in between Boston and Concord (true) probably on a noise statute violation (not true).

In addition, The Boston Globe has never owned up to its historical hysterectomy, claiming that it couldn't have reported about Paul Revere in 1775, because it wasn't even a newspaper until 1872! Well, here's a bulletin to The Boston "Right Lobe" Globe: "If you had of been there, you would have screwed it up anyway." So there!

The death of a nation

Political commentary is one of those few things that went immediately south at birth. As we just learned, the very first attempt to record and explain history to the American public was butchered by the predecessor to The Boston Globe, whatever that might have been. For the next 75 years, political commentary consisted of cartoons lampooning (from the Latin root: "to screw over") Presidents, crooks, rich politicians, and other Republicans. Cartoons were used because few people could read back in those days, and many of them were somewhat intellectually challenged, much like the people who read cartoons today.

But all of that changed in the mid 1800s with the first publication of Harper's Weekly. Harper's was one of a genre of four magazines at the time (Judge, Truth, and Life were the others) that were also long on pictures and short on tolerance. They were very successful, but after a few years they decided that ruining careers and aspirations could be raised to a new height—with new blood.

So Harper's goes to the waiver-wire and finds this crazy German named Thomas Nast. Nast was our first, almost eponymous, hard-core commentator—he was NAST-y. He could draw cartoons and say things about folks that would have gotten Don Imus fired twice.

If those of you on the Far Right and Far Left think that this country was built on the bedrock of balanced political correctness, then you need to put down The Boston Globe and pick up the pace.

Harper's full name was Harper's Weekly—A Journal of Civilization. Here are just a few examples of "civilization" American style, courtesy of Harper's: 1) The Irish were depicted as chimpanzees; 2) Catholic bishops were depicted as crocodiles eating American families, i.e., "Let Us Prey"; 3) the Chinese were referred to as John Chinaman; 4) fat people were depicted as fat, and thin people were depicted as fat if that helped sell magazines; and 5) the only "class" that was spared was the "Negroes" who were beneath the contempt of early-day ideological thought.

What's even more important is that Harper's also had a strong subscriber base in the South, and "Lordy, how'd you think those folk would take to readin' 'bout the negra problem all the dag, blame day?" (very true).

In support of both Harper's and Thomas Nast, both of them did some extraordinary reporting. Nast, with the support of Harper's, went after Boss Tweed and Tammany Hall (the Democratic machine in New York), and despite being offered $200,000 to quit, Nast kept laying the wood to them.

During that same time, The New York Times was offered $5 million not to report on the matter, and to its credit, The Times also kept the heat on 'til Tweed was arrested. During this same period, and demonstrating similar courage, The Boston Globe decided never to report on anything that might ever happen on Chappaquiddick Island, in order to protect the privacy of settlers who might go there someday.

Here's some useless trivia: Boss Tweed escaped jail, fled to Spain, and was eventually caught by the local police after Nast drew a cartoon of him, on the run, and sent it to the Spanish police (true).

Irrespective of the few instances of good, delivered by the political columnists (as we mentioned above), they were largely a real, albeit humorous, pain in the ass to anybody in public life.

And as if no surprise at all, top on their list to criticize was the President of the United States. Presidents in the 1800's were much like Presidents today—surrounded by "handlers" who explained what the President just said, but in Washington-ese, which is a second language.

However, by the beginning of the 1920's, the White House got down and dirty. Presidents had become mighty tired of being the "pee-post for petty, political polemicists." (We're not sure what that means, but it doesn't sound positive.) The Presidents had had it up to here. It was clearly time not only to "be" offensive, but to "go", on the offensive.

The White House press secretary is born!

The first White House press secretary (WHPS) was George Ackerson, who served under Herbert Hoover from 1929 until 1931. God knows—if any President ever needed a press secretary, it was Herb. Bless his heart, this goof thought that technological solutions could go a long way toward curing economic and social ills. Ha, ha. What's next? Phones you can carry around in your pocket? How avant-garde (from the French for "useless").

Apparently, these technological solutions didn't extend to preventing the Great Depression, which started on Hoover's watch. Matter of historical fact: The Great Depression didn't begin to end until another press secretary, Stephen Early, suggested that Franklin Roosevelt coin a phrase remembered to this day: "You have nothing to fear but Hoover's fat ass back in the White House." Just kidding, he really said, "You have nothing to fear, but fear itself." This was a very catchy phrase, which galvanized our country into starving to death with a smile on our face. We're going to give credit to Stephen Early, rather than Franklin Roosevelt, for this phrase, because it's clear that anybody who would marry Eleanor doesn't exactly have an eye for a catchy anything.

Since then, there have been big WHPS (Pierre Salinger—JFK) and little WHPS (Jerald F. ter Horst—Gerald Ford). No matter whether they were big or little, these guys had only one job: Re-say in unintelligible, non ethnic-baiting words what the President had just said two hours before that made him sound like he was stupid and a racist. In addition, they also had to kind of cover up little Presidential and Presidential family foibles. For example, Bill Clinton's definition of what "is" is; the Kennedy's banging on everything in Washington except the door out and Jimma Carter's brother Billy, who was a walking headline. Example of true quote: "Yessir. I'm a real Southern boy. I got a red neck, white socks, and a Blue Ribbon beer." Ronald Reagan called his wife "Mommie," and Lyndon Johnson's family turned the White House into some kind of human "elle" aviary (Lady Bird, Lucy Bird, Linda Bird), and so on and so forth.

Ladies and gentlemen of the Far Center; boys and girls everywhere; all the ships at sea: the battle lines are now drawn. We're calling it the way it is!

The President and his staff have the "bully pulpit." The political commentators have the "bully media," and all we get when we read the newspapers or watch TV is the "bully shit." Enough!

The Self-Appointed

Motto: *"We only hunt the badly wounded".*

As you recall in the "Advice to Readers" section of this book, we vowed to neither be ad hominem nor even ad wominem. With the possible exceptions of the United Nations and Eleanor Roosevelt, we have kept our promise. However, as we begin to discuss the media maggots (delete that right now) who have infested even the healthy tissue of our body politic, we may have to get, as is said in the State Department, "frank and candid." By the way, when you read that people like President Obama and President Putin had a "frank exchange of views," that means that they made each of their respective interpreters give the other the finger. In this way the Presidents can remain "diplomatic" and can enjoy dinner.

Anyway, let's get on with the issue at hand. As the term "self-appointed" indicates, these people just showed up on your figurative doorstep one day and began talking to you like you had been real good friends, for a real long time. These folks come in many guises, but they're always heavily cloaked in the raiment of wisdom, which you don't have and never will have because you are a common voter and a mean-spirited wage earner who did not go to Harvard and graduate with honors like the 91 percent of the Harvard class of 2001 did (very true). Many of these students are already on their way to post-graduate work at the Electoral College.

Who are these people, and can they be dealt with peacefully like Al-Qaeda or must Nobel Laureates be dispatched from the United Nations to have "a frank and candid exchange of views" with them? Answer: No, and, Please God, No.

These men and women—who go by the names of Coulter, Matthews, O'Reilly, Limbaugh, Maher and Williams—are hardened warriors who refuse to kill the healthy. They can hear a politician dragging a leg in the jungle from as far as a mile away. They can, and will, repeat themselves five times and only make it seem like seven. They can, and will, have more fun with the facts than a sailor on shore leave. They are well dug in, in the hardened bunkers of bias and prejudice. They can be more startling than ordering a limo and finding out your driver is Marty Feldman without corrective lenses.

Do not approach these people unless you are well armed!"

Using the crayons provided to you when you bought this book, please match the statement with the person (of course by drawing an arrow, dimwit) who said it, or who most closely resembles it.

Ann Coulter

Asks leading questions and then smirks at the answers like a schoolboy who just made a funny noise with his armpit.

Brian Williams

Said the 9/11 terrorists weren't cowards—–Americans were the cowards for lobbing bombs from 2,000 miles away.

Bill O'Reilly

Describing a Parkinson's patients suffering: "He's moving all around and shaking, and he's either faking it or he's off his medication."

Rush Limbaugh

With what can only be described as "leading edge" illustration, described another commentator as a "big, fat, lying liar."

Bill Maher

Described the widows of some 9/11 victims as "the witches of East Brunswick," who enjoyed benefiting financially from their husbands' deaths.

Chris Matthews

Closer to reasonable thought than the rest of this squad but still not exactly on the "pinnacle of the fulcrum" as he professes.

The Self-Anointed

Motto: "We 'Are' without sin; We 'Will' cast the first stone"!

You know these people—you know you know them! Remember when you were at work one day and these uninvited boogs would show up and say, "Hi, I'm from the home office—I'm here to help. "These are they!!".

Unlike the previously discussed "self-appointed," who were cloaked in the raiment of "wisdom," the self-anointed arc cloaked in the raiment of "righteousness." These folks are not necessarily smarter than you—they are just more well-connected. This is because they have been visited by a "higher authority," which you have not. And this higher authority has directed them to save the common voter—and mean-spirited wage earner—from themselves.

Although not their normal habitat, these folks also will stalk in the media jungle. However, unlike the self-appointed, they do not wish to "shoot the badly wounded"—they wish to, "wound the shooter!!" These people are usually identified as either anti-anything groups or pro-anything groups. In addition, the end always justifies the means to these people, because they have been in touch with a higher authority and, as usual, you have not. This crowd makes Machiavelli look like a pansy-ass! To these people, there is no cause so trivial that it does not trump the greater good if 1) it originated at a Bible college, 2) it originated in some god-awful African hell-hole, 3) it is championed by nine people from North Dakota who seldom bathe, or 4) it's animal, vegetable, or mineral—but not human.

Are these people walking amongst us?

When young people are growing up, they often ask for "action figures" for their birthday or Christmas. These figures represent the forceful actions of brave men and women as they preserve the American Way. When the self-anointed are growing up, they ask for **inaction figures!** There is no problem so insignificant for them that it cannot be elevated to planetary importance. They usually form thoughtful "study groups," followed by prayer for divine or intellectual guidance, and then they blow up a dam, burn down a building, or harpoon an aircraft carrier. All of which is justified, because it immediately changes the unnatural order of plodding along as a country of laws.

The self-anointed **cannot be** eliminated altogether—they can only be identified and studied with extreme caution, and from a safe distance!

Who are they? Bill Bennett, The Ninth Circuit Court of Appeals, Sierra Club, PETA, Pat Robertson, and the ACLU (American Civil Liberties Union).

Once again using the crayons provided to you, please match the statement with the person, idiot, or group who most resembles it or, God forbid, actually said it.

PETA	"Decency... decency is what your grandmother taught you. It's in your bones. You go home now. Go home and be decent people. Be decent."
Ninth Circuit Court	"By shifting the blame from... first world plunderers... to the invading hordes of immigrants... the Far Right is promoting its racist conclusions."
ACLU	"To profess that we are a 'nation under God' is identical to saying we are a 'nation under Vishnu' or a 'nation under Zeus,' or a 'nation under no God'."
Sierra Club	"Lord give us righteous judges who will not try to legislate and dominate our society. TAKE CONTROL LORD. We ask for additional vacancies on the court."
Bill Bennett	"These actions are a cruel travesty." We should "engage in a in a new campaign to EDUCATE WOLVES... that non-animal protein is better suited for health."
Pat Robertson	"As badly as boys in our society need role models and meaningful after-school activities, we all should hope that the Boy Scouts choose the latter."

John P. Broach

The Self-Absorbed

Motto: "I thought PolySci was a food additive!"

This group will align themselves with almost any cause célèbre (French for, "much photographed annoyance") because they realize that the only bad publicity is no publicity. They are cloaked in the Burberry of "dense fog."

According to their publicist (by the way, if you don't have a publicist in Hollywood, then you're still making soap commercials), they have been "in between scripts for the last ten years" because they have not been challenged by the message the screenwriter is trying to convey. Translation: They are complete has-beens.

Like all of our Presidential candidates, the self-absorbed have deeply held beliefs that they have held, deeply, since they were just wee little up and coming stars. This helps you, the common voter and mean-spirited wage earner, understand why, once again, this third of the three asymptotes is better than you. You never had deeply held beliefs, held deeply since you were eight years old, and as a consequence you can't run for office or appear on TV. For those of you who have never come to grips with this reality, you may now begin to grieve—and then heal—but please make it quick.

Unlike all of our Presidential candidates, these people frequently cry spontaneously, apparently for no reason. This now answers your question as to why they are cloaked in the raiment of dense fog. The combination of dry southern California air and all this crying creates a low weather system around these people, which leads to very dense fog. The other reason is—they're just naturally dense.

The self-absorbed interject themselves into politics because when you are "in between scripts" about car chases, you have the time to reflect and have large thoughts. Once these thoughts are distilled into definable action items, the self-absorbed assemble photographers and announce a plan to reduce polar ice-cap melting by adopting a baby from the Sudan.

When it comes to predictability, these people are as interchangeable as a skate key. They are typically neither Far Right nor Far Left—just Far Removed. They feel "called" to politics and to its study.

To underscore their gift for politics, in a recent (and Far Center) random survey conducted on Rodeo Drive, 10 out of 10 respondents answered correctly that 1) Princess Di was the Queen of England and 2) Mother Teresa was the Phi Delta House Mom at UCLA. To paraphrase Winston Churchill (badly), "Never have so many, given so little, to accomplish nothing."

When in the media jungle, they prefer to move in large groups, surrounded by a gaggle of assorted misfits who were borrowed, the day before, from Central Casting. They are generally not a truculent sort (French for, "to surrender") and prefer to "hug" and "stroke" their prey as opposed to the self-appointed, who "mug" and "poke."

We are unable to match people and organizations with their quotes, as shown previously. This is because, they are all alike and cannot be differentiated!"

The Centers' Conclusion

If you wish to understand and effectively deal with the self-appointed and self-anointed, go to their breeding grounds and lay traps of style, class, and intelligence. These are their natural enemies. Once they are born, it is impossible to eradicate them––this must be done "in utero" (Latin for, in wombo).

As for the self-absorbed, the answer is simple. As a country, we spend as much on movies each year as the entire planet spends on the United Nations ($20 billion each year). They aren't hurting anyone, they seldom leave LA, and they are an entertaining sort in their own way.

CENTER PIECE 6

The Federal Reserve System (Fed)

Motto: "We speak entirely in tongues".

Former Fed Chairman Alan Greenspan:
"If you understood what I said,
you weren't listening close enough."
Janet Yellen Current Fed Chairwomanish: "What did he say?"

Although no longer the Fed Chairman, we picture Alan Greenspan because he was the first to teach us to "speak in tongues".

"Speaking in tongues" comes from the Greek word "glossalalia," which means "to talk like a politician" (not strictly true, but mostly true). Speaking in tongues is normally associated with evangelists who have deeply religious experiences around the offering plate in a large tent in Oklahoma. The U.S. government often has a similar experience around its offering plate, each year around April 15th. This, of course, is what ties the Federal Reserve System to evangelicals. Both love your money; both love to talk about your money; both become totally incoherent when asked about their money. We should probably move on from here; such comparisons are only going to inflame the Federal Reserve.

Many people have preconceived notions about what the Federal Reserve (Fed) is and what it does. You're probably wrong on all counts. Let's use the frequently asked question (FAQ) device to clear some air.

1. Is the Fed a government agency?... *Yeah, kind of.*
2. Does the Fed print my money?... *No.*
3. Does this organization have goals and objectives like the mean-spirited wage earners who pay their salary?... *No.*
4. Do they have a "boss"? Their "boss" is Congress. *Therefore the answer is... No.*
5. Is the Fed the reason I lost my ass in the "tech bubble" and can no longer afford my home?... *Yes.*
6. So they have no purpose. Then why don't we just call them Vice Presidents or First Ladies?... *Those names were already taken.*

Why do we have a Federal Reserve System, and do other strong economies, like Montenegro, have one as well?

Money really began to catch on in this country in 1862, with the Legal Tender Act. At the time, the United States was engaged in the American Civil War, or "decidetocide" (this is a new word, which means to kill yourself and your countrymen in the name of future generations). Unlike our current—and highly successful—efforts in the Middle East, there were no taxes to finance well-thought-out armed destruction in the name of democracy. Therefore, in order to fund the cost of the Civil War, the U.S. Department of Treasury printed attractive green bills with not so attractive pictures (think George Washington) on them and told everyone that they were as good as gold. If you wanted to exchange them, all you had to do was go to the bank and ask for gold equal to your currency. Very efficient (and very true).

In response, the Confederacy decided to print its own currency to finance its share of the Civil War and told everyone that Confederate money was backed by cotton (true). The problem, of course, was that the Confederacy didn't tell anybody where to go to get their money redeemed for cotton (also true). In addition, and if that wasn't enough, all Confederate bills had pictures of happy slaves bailing cotton on them (believe it or not, this is true), which was one step beneath looking at George Washington's ugly puss.

Here's the final problem! Enterprising northerners immediately began counterfeiting the Confederate currency and within a couple of years it was so worthless that "Manor-house massa couldn't even buy hisself a proper slave, much less a bail a cotton. Lands-a-goshen, what is this world coming to?" Long story short, neither the Confederates nor the Confederates' currency, ever quite caught on.

Although not completely apparent to the Deep South **to this day**, the Confederacy lost the war, and the "greenback" became king.

From the end of the Civil War until 1873, things went along swimmingly. Then in 1873, the Bank of Philadelphia declared bankruptcy; this created a domino effect throughout the country, which put America in a deep funk (depression) until 1877. Then in 1893, everyone decided to take the government up on its offer to redeem their currency for gold. Guess what? You are correct. Not enough gold to cover the green. Back in the funk again. Then in 1907, it happened again. However, this one was the biggie. It was so big, it was called the "Bankers' Panic."

Until now, when there was a financial catastrophe––as long as it was confined to American men and women who brought nothing to the party but votes and honest labor––we could live with their misery, as long as it was from a safe distance. **But not this one––no siree!** Banks were big stuff, run by important financiers (Latin for, 'crook') whose money lubricated the very machinery of commerce. To let these brave Americans suffer might eventually lead to a Great Depression around 1930, or sometime like that, and **by gum, we won't let that happen!** Therefore, the U.S. government decided to do something that only the truly gifted financial mind could have conceived––they created **another** bank. But this wasn't just any old bank. It was the banks' bank. *The Federal Reserve System is born!*

When I grow up, I would like to either be a farm implement or the Chairman of the Federal Reserve. What is your advice?

As you might suspect, a strong background in **usefulness**—where the effort expended is in direct proportion to a clear and predictable outcome—is where you should concentrate your career goals. I suggest a garden hoe! Since its inception in 1913, the Fed has had 15 chairpeople. Each made A's in their economics classes—**and** nobody had ever heard of them before they became Chairman of the Fed.

That's all you need to know, and I'm not going to tell you anything else about them.

How is the 'Fed' organized, and what does it do?

The Fed is made up of 12 banks called Federal Reserve Banks. These banks are located conveniently through out the United States, so that, as with all government agencies, if you have an issue or a query, all you have to do is pop in and say, "Why did you just ruin my life by increasing the interest rate on my loan?"

The role of the Federal Reserve is simple. It is to ensure an economy that moves along smoothly and with confidence. Since 1913, the Fed has controlled, tightly and thoughtfully, the amount of money that is available in our country, so that huge swings like the Great Depression, sparked by the crash of '29 (which cost several trillion dollars in today's money) and the disastrous collapse of the market in 2000-2001 (which cost several trillion dollars in today's money) would never happen. **Memo to Fed: You're 0 for 2.**

Those of us in the Center are not huge fans of the Fed. We're old-school people who want to understand what a government agency does for us, how they do it, and why I don't feel better after they did it.

*Got "**FED**" lately?*

Here's a bulletin, Feddie: As a country, we may no longer have "bank panics" or even "bank runs," but I get the "trots" now and then. So how am I better off?

As discussed earlier, the twelve Federal Reserve Banks act as the operating arm of the Federal Reserve System. If the Fed is dissatisfied with how the economy is going, they will work through their Federal Reserve Banks to either increase or decrease interest rates. For example, if the Fed wants to slow the economy down a wee little, it will raise interest rates. The Fed does this by instructing its member banks to immediately call upon all the banks in their region to issue an interest rate **"SOHON"**. Within seconds, interest rates are higher. A "SOHON" is the American economic equivalent of a fatwa. "SOHON" stands for "Screw Over Home Owners Now." The member banks then call you and say, 1) your adjustable rate mortgage just tripled 2) it's now going to cost the rough equivalent of Sierra Leone's GDP to send your kids to college and/or 3) "NO—no one wants to buy your home! What idiot would borrow money at this rate to buy your home, which **just** decreased in value, because of what **I just** did to you?"

Conversely, if the Fed wishes to **lower** interest rates, your banker is usually at an ethics seminar in Phoenix and will get back to you in a couple of months.

Excuse me! How can this be? Explanation: until the publication of this superbly researched book, the answer was not known. However, let it **now** be known: Once hired, all bankers enter into the "Secret Society of the 3-9-3." Each banker is required to go to their regional Federal Reserve Bank and repeat the following oath: "I, [state your tight-ass banker name], do solemnly swear to abide by the covenants of the 3-9-3 Society, even if it means foreclosing on my grandma's home and putting her burdensome old backside on the bricks. To wit: I will borrow money from the Fed at 3 percent. I will lend that same money to mean-spirited wage earners at 9 percent. I will be on the golf course at 3 each day."

There are other ways the Fed helps out you and the economy. If it wants to put more money in America's economic system, it buys certain government securities. If it wants to take money out of the system (for example, the month before you put your house on the market), it sells government securities. The Fed influences monetary supply and policy in many other ways, but to explain them would take you, the reader, to the absolute limits of tedium.

The Federal Reserve Chairman meets with his "boss," the U.S. Congress **twice a year!** Now that's accountability! During that meeting, things are said that you are too dumb to understand. Many of the members of Congress listen attentively, with furrowed and studied brows. Some scratch their chin in a wise manner, suggesting full comprehension and approval. Occasionally, they will turn to each other and nod knowingly. If you only got a C in economics, and graduated from the Electoral College, you'd do the same thing.

In addition, many of the meetings with Congress are held behind closed doors, and the transcripts are not released for five years (true). This type of secretive behavior makes many people distrust the Fed in general and bankers in particular. One of the first of these folks was President Andrew Jackson— way back in 1832. Addressing a delegation of **bankers no less**, (and presumably wearing some sort of protective vest), he said, "You are a den of vipers and thieves. I intend to rout you out, and by the eternal God, I **will** rout you out" (true).

It's easy to misunderstand the Fed; it happens to everyone. Matter of fact, when President Obama was much younger and looking for a place to do his military service (say what?), he originally applied to be a Federal Reservist.

I'm depressed. Can you cheer me up with knowledge?

OK. Here's an easy quiz that will make you appear smart to your friends. Pay attention, Presidential candidates. Using the green crayon provided to you when you purchased this book, please circle the appropriate answer.

True or false: **The total value of all U.S. bills in existence today is approximately $1.0 trillion.**

What is the best way to dispose of your worn-out U.S. currency?
   A) Give it to the Federal Reserve, which shreds it and replaces your worn currency with new.
   B) Give it to my stock broker; he can destroy anything.

How long does a hundred-dollar bill last before it wears out?
   A) 89 months
   B) 89 seconds, if in the hands of Congress.

The largest note ever printed was the $100,000 bill. Whose picture was out?
   A) Alex de Tocqueville
   B) The Clinton Foundation
   C) Koch Brothers
   D) None of the above

What happened to the $500, $1,000, $5,000 and $10,000 notes?
    A) Somebody gave them to my stock broker.
    B) Who cares? I never had one.
    C) Discontinued in 1969 because of A) and B) above.

The Center's Conclusion

Facts, data and bended knee have not softened the heart of the Fed. Their door is always open, and their mind is always closed. Those of us in the Center believe that the only way to reach this "apparatchik" (Russian for "stooge") is through a dulcet lyric (Latin for, "song"). We now summon up the ghost of John Lennon, who in 1969 gave us the song "All We Are Saying Is Give Peace a Chance." In this same vein we call upon the Federal Reserve to "Give **Gold** a Chance." The Center has a song in its heart.

Once again, lift your voices to Washington. Stand up immediately and sing:

*All we are saying... is give **gold** a chance.*
*My wallet is empty... with the Feds' **dollar** dance.*
High Bishop Yellen, we need a grubstake,
*Return to the **gold** coin, and give us a break.*

Alright everybody, arms in the air. Second stanza, don't be afraid, be proud, sing **out loud** and sway if you wish:

> *Answer our prayer please, and throw us a **bone**,*
> *A piece of the action, like a little **bullion***
> *Speak-a da English, a language we **get**,*
> *An ounce of pure gold, ma'am, not a pound of **Fed shit***

We, in the Center, are going to go with Voltaire (1694-1778), who said: "Paper money eventually returns to its intrinsic value––zero!"

CENTER PIECE 7

The Father... The Son... The "Holy Shit"!
(FBI)   (CIA)   IRS)

Our Motto: We're on top of everything, including you.

FBI, CIA, and IRS. Rearrange the letters and they still don't spell anything (don't bother, I tried for two hours).

The FBI was established in 1908, largely by a U.S. Attorney General named Charles Bonaparte. Bonaparte, unwilling to wait for the slow wheels of **Due Process** to get rolling, decided that he would organize a bunch of detectives who worked directly for him and were accountable directly to nobody, and would tell them to get out there and do the Lords' work. He reckoned, correctly, that we were still a lawless country, divided into States that didn't particularly love each other, seldom communicated about things of mutual interest, and who fifty years earlier had tried to destroy each other over what color went best with a new country. (This is totally unlike the Middle-East, today, which needs our intervention).

As good fortune would have it, J. Edgar Hoover was also thirteen years old at the time the FBI was conceived. Beady-eyed and sneaky, history would demand that Hoover be groomed for an important position in government and it was felt that the FBI would be just the ticket!

The CIA was established in 1947 by Harry Truman. The purpose, surprise surprise, was to collect information on hostile governments who had lot's of bushes to hide behind. We are currently not doing well in our Middle East anti-terrorism efforts because not one of these countries has signed on to the 'Sprinkler Round' as adopted by the United Nations. The 'Sprinkler Round' requires all countries to have proper sprinkling systems so that bushes large enough to hide behind and take pictures can begin to grow.

Anyway, the military **AND** the State Department **AND** the FBI were all very opposed to the establishment of the CIA (true). After all.... for years these organizations had been buying the Brownie cameras to take pictures of people who were taking pictures of them and it wasn't fair, to have to share. That's why, even today September 11, reminds us of the following: "Would a phone call between all you clowns, have been too much to ask?"

The IRS was established by the Revenue Act of 1862 to finance that little war over which color goes best with America, that we just spoke about, above.

Reader, I agree with you completely! All this time, **I also** thought the IRS was created by some President I hated, in order to penalize mean-spirited-wage-earners for having been born. Nobody hates Abe Lincoln, and he was the one who created the IRS. Moral of story: We have an IRS, because our ancestors, **yesterday**, hated each other worse, than we hate the IRS, **today**! What goes 'round, comes 'round.

The FBI

"Our 'Hoover' sucks more than yours".
Cross-cultural communications between the CIA and the FBI

J. Edgar Hoover was the FBI's first and longest tenured Director. He only fell one year short of Strom Thurmond's record for having grossly over-stayed his welcome. Strom was around for 49 years as a U.S. Senator and J. Edgar for 48 years as Director. Isn't history wonderful? Do you know what else these two dinosaurs had in common? Well, apparently after Strom's death it was proved that he had been Strumming some of the household help ('help' only comes in one color in South Carolina) and fathered a child. In the case of Hoover, he apparently altered his birth records to conceal that someone in the family may have been, shall we say, darkish. (Read, Millie McGhee's 'Secrets Uncovered').

After Hoover's death, a law was immediately passed (true) that FBI Directors could only serve for ten years. Hoover lasted as long as he did because he had a steamer trunk of dirt on just about everybody on the planet and especially Presidents. Nixon tried to fire him twice and backed down both times. Truman, Kennedy and Johnson also wanted to can him, but had no appetite for what they thought would be some serious, political brain damage.

Hoover's antics while he was in charge, make the Fidels' singing sea shell episode pale (explained later) to insignificance. He spied on Gene Autry, Elvis Presley, Groucho Marx and Lou Costello among others. Those of us in the Center really like Gene Autry. We liked his horse, Champion. We even liked his wife, as long as it was in small doses. Gene Autry created the *Cowboy Code* for the kids, that said things like,

"You never shoot first", "Be gentle with children and the elderly" "Don't be intolerant of race or religion" and many more. No wonder Hoover hated him.

He also had extensive files on John Lennon and the Yoko-meister. It was clear to Hoover that this unholy 'union' could only breed subversion and these two needed to be closely watched (Hoover called in sick the day they taught Anthropology). He ran agents out of the FBI whom he thought were 'pinheads' or 'truck drivers'. He instituted the 'dirty tricks' programs, trying to discredit anybody available but mostly 'negro radicals' like Martin Luther King and subversive Hollywood-types. Those of us in the Center believe that Hoover and Joe McCarthy had a side bet of $5 on who could gum up the works worse under the guise of truth, justice and the American way. Apparently Hoover won because the FBI headquarters in Washington, D.C. is named the J. Edgar Hoover building. Conversely, McCarthy's heirs are still hoping for a little footprint at Grauman's Chinese Theater, assuming bygones can be bygones.

Hoover died in 1977. For the last forty years, the FBI has been recovering nicely and doing some spectacular work on behalf of the nation. I don't know exactly what because when I called, the lady on the phone wouldn't tell me. I do know that she sounded nice and interested, unlike the American Airlines ticket reservation lady who I called the day before, (September 25 at @ 4:00P.M., MST) who was the most un-nice and unhelpful lady in the world. Apparently we now know two things: 1) Hoover Happens 2) American Airlines Happens.

The Central Intelligence Agency (CIA)

**"Oh what a tangeled web we weave,
When once we become a political dweeb".**

The CIA can trace its' roots all the way back to 5 B.C., when Roman Emperor Augustus created the Praetorian Guard. 'Praetorian' comes from the word 'Praetor' which means "Commanding General". Commanding General's, back in those days used to pick particularly well qualified guards from the ranks of the foot soldiers, to guard their tents at night. This may be the reason why we refer to CIA Agents as 'spooks', even to this day. Their job was to run around the Generals' tent at night and scare people away. People who didn't scare away easily were killed and then questioned under psychedelic drugs...later it was determined by the CIA, that the reverse procedure would yield roughly the same results.

The Praetorian Guard was a useful, political tool to many Emperors, who correctly trusted no one, especially their best friends. Emperors decided that The Guard could also be useful if they were deployed in very stealthy ways to kill political enemies. This may well have been the first 'dirty tricks department', which was later perfected by the FBI in the 1960's. Sometimes The Guard would place olive oil on the marble steps leading down to the privy of people the Emperor suspected of being disloyal and then bang their spoons together in the middle of the night, until the person woke up and went to the bathroom. Other times, The Guard would send them exploding harlots. Like the CIA today, the list of mischievousness was limited only by the imagination. Anyway, as time went on, these guys became an unpredictable embarrassment **(giving us conclusive proof that history repeats itself)** and Diocletian disbanded them in 300A.D.

The CIA, that you know and love today, was created in 1947 by Congress. As with all things created by Congress, swift and decisive exorcism is usually performed and you are not harmed and you never hear from it again. This did not happen with the CIA.

As a matter of fact the CIA has been playing an important role to each President since Harry Truman by reading them what was reported in the New York Times two weeks earlier, ironically this is not the case for Obama…he's **on** the editorial staff of the New York Times. In the case of Truman, the CIA never told him (because they didn't know) that the Soviet Union had developed the Atom Bomb in 1949 until we all got to see it in Red Square (true). In the case of George H.W. Bush (George the First) we didn't have any idea that Iraq was going to invade Kuwait until after it had happened. (Let's stop here for a moment of Far Center poignancy. Guess who was the CIA Director between 1976-1977? YES, George H.W. Bush. Once again. What goes 'round, comes 'round.)

In order to not be completely negative, Dwight Eisenhower said that the CIA during his presidency had left a "legacy of ashes" (true) and Richard Nixon, who misused The Agency more than anybody, referred to them as "clowns reading newspapers." (Also true).

We don't know what the CIA does or where it does it. That's probably OK, only the Far Left would think it was nifty to sit down and tell everybody who we were spying on. We also don't know how many people do what we don't know they're doing and how much money they spend doing it. That's classified and also OK, I guess. But what we do know is that, as a country, we don't like to be laughed at. PLEASE PAY CLOSE ATTENTION. In the early 1960's we tried to assassinate Fidel Castro. He didn't like us and we didn't like him. (Things have clearly changed since they are now our 51st state). So the CIA sends him an exploding sea shell so that when he put it up to his ear to hear the ocean it would go Boom and blow his head off. HONEST TO GOD, THIS IS THE TRUTH. Unless you are the CIA, you just can't make crap like this up. Aside from the fact that the plot seems to have been hatched by Bill Belichick.....did it ever occur to the CIA that a man who had lived on a Caribbean island in the middle of the ocean probably didn't need the thrill of holding some Conch shell up to his ear to hear the ocean. The conversation in Cuba, between Fidel and his brother, Raul would have probably gone like this:

> **Fidel:** *"Hey Raul, look at the large, singing sea shell that somebody mistakenly left on our dining room table. Que pasa?"*
>
> **Raul:** *"Fidel, my man, I haven't seen one of those for three whole minutes"*
>
> **Fidel:** *"Raul, I will now put it up to my ear to hear the ocean, which I also have not heard for three whole minutes."*
>
> **Raul:** *"Watch out, Fidel, there may be a bomb in that shell, placed there by those lop-eyed morons from the North.*
>
> **Fidel:** *"OK, let's just mail it back to them, postage due. Ha, Ha, Hee, Hee. By the way, the revolution is going bueno."*

To make matters worse, it was widely reported that the CIA had employed the good offices of the Mafia to carry out this adventure. Those of us in the Far Center, deal not in innuendo and idle rumor! Therefore, I personally contacted the spokesperson for the Mob, Angelino "Smack Talk" Scarpelli in Bayoone, New Jersey to get her side of the story. Her response was as follows: "The reports of the Mafias' involvement in this affair were a big hit in the press, and a big hit with dagophobes. But I would just like to say that if this were our 'hit', we wouldn't have screwed it up."

Memo to President Obama and succeeding Presidents: When you get your daily Intelligence Briefing, see to it that it is presented, JOINTLY, by the Director of the CIA and the Director of the FBI, not some intermediary who is unaccountable for their information. After a few sessions it will become clear that these two still don't speak. Like the gallows, there is nothing like a little humiliation and ownership to focus a mans' mind. It is clear that these children do not play well in OUR backyard.... Your intervention will be greatly appreciated.

The IRS

"You lean on us....We gonna lien on you".

In case of an IRS Audit,
1) Break glass 2) Move quickly
3) You're screwed.

Of course you don't know who the head of the IRS is, reader. If it was your son, would you want everybody to know? Actually the head of the IRS was Lois Lerner but she took the 5th and then the night train out of town. The current head of the IRS is John Koskinen.

Before we launch into our factual diatribe, the Far Center in general, and the author of this book in particular, would like to point out that the IRS, **HAS NEVER, AND WILL NEVER**, do anything wrong. These brave men and women can pistol-whip a deduction, pencil-whip a tax haven and horse-whip a farmer who just lost his entire sorghum crop and dared to write off the loss. I would also like to point out that, although not a Mormon, I regularly tithe to the Internal Revenue Service, an additional 10% of what I owe, in order to help this fine organization meet any of its' budgetary shortfalls.

Apparently, **and unfortunately**, there are others in government, and elsewhere, who do not share my unbridled admiration for the IRS. Congress and roughly 217 million taxpayers, to name two.

As mentioned earlier, the IRS was established in 1862 because we had a war to finance. Matter of fact, if you made between, $600-$10,000 you paid 3% income tax. That was fairly adult money back in those days and went a long way. Particularly so, since we didn't have Haliburton contracts and $700 Department of Defense toilet seats. Then in 1878 the government got rid of the income tax and replaced it with a tax on tobacco and alcohol. Historically speaking, the reader may be interested to know that at almost this exact time (give or take a few years) the Mormon Church enrollment, just went gangbusters. I mean, talk about a no-brainer. These guys were a walking tax dodge. They didn't drink or smoke. Although we are a tolerant country, there is a limit to everything, especially where money is concerned. The government re-instituted the income tax in 1913. Now the Mormons are stuck with no booze, no weed and are paying taxes out the kazoo, like the rest of us, just to feel absolutely miserable every day.

Please note: Senator Harry Reid is a Mormon, and for the life of me I've never seen a more miserable human. He's even taken to wearing sunglasses…in-doors.

In 1943, our country was embroiled in WWII and guess what? Like the Civil War, we were a little short. So the government instituted the 'Withholding Tax'. That's the one where your paycheck is automatically reduced by a tax, **before** your kids get to make their deductions.

Right now many of you are beginning to form a knee-jerk, wholly negative opinion of the IRS. I will help you mature this feeling later, but for right now, you should know that when the Withholding Tax was instituted, Americas' population grew overnight, by 19 million out of nowhere. **Center Guy, would you stop right there? I don't understand and I don't know what this has to do with the taxation of 'mean-spirited wage earners'.** Explanation: Imagine the unpatriotic gall!! 19 million Americans earning wages and not sharing them with the IRS. In the words of a famous American Indian, the IRS was plenty pissed. I can also tell you, that from 1943 until about 1970, the IRS raised taxpayer abuse to Abu Ghraib proportions. This was Payback, Mel Gibson style.

In response to this, the government began to swiftly address this growing scourge (as is their wont) of rogue agents having their way with unsuspecting taxpayers, and occasionally their wives. For the next twenty years, congress passed Tax Reform Acts, Tax Reconciliation Acts, tax increases, tax decreases and in general this was just plain a very taxing time in our history. All these changes in the tax code confused the IRS, which made them madder and meaner.

Enough!! We must have Congressional hearings and we must have them now.

In the hearings which followed, before the Senate Finance Committee in the late 1990's, the testimony was overwhelming that the IRS had abused their position, covered up their abuses and generally enjoyed being abusive. In 1998, Senator William Roth, Chairman of the Senate Finance Committee addressed the IRS as follows: "If history has taught us anything about the IRS, it is that, despite past efforts to reform the agency, it has consistently succeeded in falling back into a pattern of mismanagement, abuse and inefficiency." (For my money, he could just as easily been talking about the FBI).

After a long litany of tales of the IRS's tax muggery, buggery, thuggery and occasional 'stoning' to break the monotony, the **Taxpayers Bill of Rights** was passed. This Bill shifted the burden of proof from the taxpayer to the IRS. Imagine, even in 1998, we still had an agency, and a law, which assumed you were guilty until proven innocent. I don't think anything has changed in the IRS's heart.

There isn't really much more to say. If we were all honest, we wouldn't need an IRS to keep us honest. Far Left alert! Making everybody honest, besides loving each other, should be your next priority.

The Centers' Conclusion

We're speechless!!

CENTER PIECE 8

War Defeated

"Annual 'Peace Champion Series' Replaces War".

In a bold move to defeat war but maintain the very best of country-on-country hatred, the Far Center has now petitioned

U.N. Secretary General Ban Ki Moon to immediately institute the annual "Peace Championship Series" or PCS.

Leveraging from the undeniable popularity, accuracy, and finality of a good play off series, the United Nations will now consider going where it has never gone before, to a conclusion! At the moment of this writing, it is rumored that Ban Ki and what will shortly be known as the U.N. WarKeepers are poring over a white paper, presented by the Far Center, which totally overhauls outdated, poorly orchestrated, and unacceptably spontaneous conflict around the world. Reached at the Far Sited Center (the site for the Far Center) located in the windowless basement of the Kansas City Federal Reserve Bank, the Far Center spokesperson, Mr. Yoda, had this to say, "Powerful shit, proposal this is."

Reader, as we always do, let's summarize this dramatic, unfolding story and then get into the specifics.

Summary

The American Football series is held every year in January in America, which decides who is the champion college football team for the rest of the year. The two teams in this game obviously had to beat everyone else, in—and without—their respective leagues. Rankings of each team are conducted weekly by outside observers based on performance against opponents, win/loss record, and other variables. Multiple criteria, administered by impartial judges, are used to evaluate these teams. At the conclusion of the football season you end up with the two strongest teams, and they play a game against each other. Whoever wins is the Champ. It's winner-take-all, end of story, grieve and begin to heal!

Those of you readers who are still awake can immediately grasp the implications of this system as applied to world war. For example, outside judges may concede that France has won its respective league, the "European Disunion," but their strength of schedule just wasn't enough to rank them consistently high during the year. I mean c'mon, the Far Center could take Holland, Belgium and Italy all in one day with a threatening hand gesture.

Historical sidebar: European Disunion was originally abbreviated as the EDs, but the Germans thought this was an insult since they've have had a hard-on for everybody in Europe since 1900.

PCS (Peace Championship Series) Proposal

World War Playoffs (or PCS if you must) will begin each year on January 1 and conclude promptly on March 16t. **STOP. Why not just round it off to March 15ᵗʰ?**

Because, March 15ᵗʰ is the Ides of March, the day Julius Caesar was murdered and is therefore thought to be a day that foretells doom. We are foretelling Peace. We just don't want to get our idea mixed up with a day that sounds bad, that's all. When **you** write **your** book, **you** can make it on March 14ᵗʰ for all I care.

On March 16ᵗʰ, a winner will be decided, planetary strife will be over, and by mandate, peace will prevail until December 31ˢᵗ. Wars between March 17ᵗʰ and December 31ˢᵗ are strictly forbidden. However, in the six weeks leading up to the start of World War on January 1ˢᵗ, the U.N. will turn a blind eye to those countries who wish to engage in saber rattling and name calling. For example, if France was looking to be highly rated in the European Disunion League (EDL), sometime around November 15ᵗʰ an editorial in the Paris *La Monde* suggesting that the Germans were still a bunch of unreconstructed, Nazi bastards would be a nice way to get the attention of the WarKeepers who might rank France highly in the EDL going into the season.

Does this idea have legs, or what? Think of it. Manageable World War, limited to 2.5 months per year, versus our current 12 months per year. And when I say peace, I mean Peace! None of this internecine crap (French for "American Civil War"). None of this Robert Mugabe "I'm beneath the world's radar" because we are a poor African nation that doesn't allow Hollywood types to adopt our babies. None of this negotiating with men in white dresses and sensible sandals. I mean PEACE, with a capital P, which rhymes with P, which stands for another word that starts with P.

Since we are not yet a perfect world, the Far Center anticipates that, on occasion, there may be some backsliding among certain countries which have an acquired taste for plunder and mayhem and just can't let go of the past. **Be forewarned!** Backsliding will result in a **very** strongly worded rebuke, on official United Nations stationery, from an important person at the U.N., which will remain part of your permanent record, permanently, or until you are accepted into the rehab unit where Hollywood types go.

Please walk us through this remarkable proposal, which could only have been conceived by a genius

In order to get everyone at each other's throat in a simultaneous and collegial manner, the Far Center advocates dividing the planet into six Tectonic Leagues. (Tectonic is defined as an "earthlike deformity, or fault line." The Far Center has no trouble finding plenty of fault with these folks:) Those leagues are as follows:

- All-Hezbollah League

- European Disunion
- Gang of Eight
- Nada Gratas
- "Stans" Around
- League of Their Own

All-Hezbollah League (AHL)

Although not historically accurate, we are going to lump a number of countries into this league because in their heart they all think alike. 1) Hezbollah means "party of God." Since your God was not invited to this "party" then you are a diseased infidel who should be blown up. Remember, there is only one true God. If you don't believe that just ask the Mormons, the Catholics, the Hindus, the Muslims, the Buddhists, the Jews, the Protestants, and the Robertsons (Pat and DeDe that is). 2) Hezbollah hates Israel, and by extension the U.S., and therefore by further extension, anybody who likes either of us. 3) Hezbollah loves everybody who hates us, which means their Christmas card list is very long.

How can I identify an All-Hezbollah, from your run-of-the-mill, poorly bathed nomad? AHL's can be identified as follows: 1) White robes are appropriate dress year-round, as long as it is accompanied by open-toed sandals. 2) More men holding hands than on a spring day in South Beach. 3) Large groups of men who can form a menacing crowd spontaneously and begin chanting in unison, the same thing, over and over. 4) People carrying signs in English that read, "Sush Bucks" and so does "Amabo." 5) Apparently, men with endless time to walk around and be filmed hating "Amerael" (a new word meaning the evil cojoining of America and Israel.)

Please list these countries so that the United Nations can begin a strongly worded rebuke. And then tell me why you don't like them: Answer 1) Iran, Iraq, Syria, Yemen, Saudi Arabia (sometimes), Palestine (whatever and wherever that is), Sudan, Ethiopia, and two "open slots" for Tunisia and Libya on a revolving basis.

Far Center conclusion and handicap. We believe that Saudi Arabia will walk away with this League in a heartbeat, and it's not about oil. It's about nomenclature! Nobody has ever won a war with a tedious, hard-to-pronounce name. We won all our big wars with people who had first names like Harry and George (twice). Russia had Ivan. The Huns had Attila. Japan lost because their guy was named Hirohito. Sounds more like a sandwich than a Samurai to me! So do you think a goob with a name like Hassan Rouhani (Iran) can win anything? No, of course not. It doesn't rhyme with anything. Plus, all the men in Iran are mad as hell because they married somebody in a burka thinking they were getting Lindsay Lohan and ended up with something that looked more like a poorly shaved Paul Wolfowitz! There is no fire in the loins of this squad. They're gutted emotionally.

How about Iraq? They have nothing left to invade with. We blew it all up. Poof, gone-zo.

Syria? Can't win, because their President is ugly and looks like Charlie Chaplin in a neck brace.

It's Saudi all the way in this league, but I've got to warn you, they will go out in the first "non-league" skirmish, probably against the Gang of Eight.

European Disunion League (EDLs)

From day to day, nobody is really sure who the hell is in or out of this league. It's roughly known as Europe, but then they've added a few countries, and then a couple of the countries that were added said "no"; and then some said "yes" and then later voted "no"; and then finally they had to add the Legacy countries, like Italy, which only made the whole thing laughable. The only way to describe who's in and who's out of this league is to invoke Winston Churchill in his Iron Curtain speech when he said, "From Stettin' in the Baltic to Trieste in the Adriatic an Iron Curtain has descended." This roughly defines Europe as running from the yak-loving Scandinavians in the north to the turban-wearing Turks in the South.

The only way to define the EDLs properly is by defining their chemical properties, because although Germany is in the EDL today and that may change over time. Therefore, who may be in or out of the EDL in five years is totally unknowable. What is knowable, and therefore predictable, is how these countries have historically behaved when faced with adversity. Finally, understanding these countries' DNA will also help the Far Center handicap and predict future pugilistic success.

Okay, how do we identify these countries which have brought us poor hygiene, month light savings time (August does not exist in Europe), and nasty-ass taxi drivers?

- Countries who gave up **after** receiving a sharply worded and threatening email
- Countries who have been invaded and immediately gave up
- Countries who like countries who give up

- Countries who were just standing around and gave up
- France

Mr. Far Center guy, who do you predict out of this league will go all the way? We in the Far Center, initially believed that either France or Germany were odds-on to take this one to the house. Why? France, with its election of Francois Hollande, seems to have lost their, how do you say, *le tissue du testiculaire*. Germany on the other hand is 0 for 2 and really poised to break into that "W" column.

However, the Far Center is going this year with... Switzerland. Yes, you heard us right, Switzerland. Here's our reasoning. The Swiss have the largest standing army per capita of any country in Europe (true). Everybody has to serve in the armed forces at one time or another, and that means good bench strength. They have the military element of surprise. Not only does everybody think they are neutral, they also think the Swiss are neutered. When Germany falls to the Swiss, all of Europe will collapse because German women have very large, muscular thighs and the Swiss will ride these women into battle against Italy and other countries who like to nap after lunch. What a slam dunk! Take it to the bank. Bet the farm.

The Gang of Eight League (GEL)

Please cut to the chase! Who are these people, and do they all share a remarkably close, physical resemblance?
Answer 1: The Gang of Eight (GEL) claims the following countries: Myanmar, Thailand, Viet Nam, Cambodia, Malaysia, Taiwan, Philippines, and Singapore.

Answer 2: Only to the finely tuned eye of the Far Right. These little buggers are definitely in play! They are going to "gel" in 2016 as their eponymous acronym (that's GEL for the Far Right) would imply. They will do this by employing what will come to be known as the Great Eight Gambit. No one but the Far Center sees this coming. Here's how it's likely to play out and why we, in the Far Center, are so high on the GEL taking it to the EDLs in the first round of inter-league play.

In a clever international feint, Thailand will invade itself and be defeated. The news of this will be prominently reported on page 5 of *The New York Times'* Sunday "Style" section, and the United Nations will prepare a sharp rebuke but forget to send it. Simultaneously, and at almost the same time, Taiwan in the north and Malaysia to the south will disguise their entire standing armies to resemble German tourists looking for a good time in Bangkok. Both countries will use this clever "pincer" movement to occupy Thailand. This **seemingly** hostile act will go completely unnoticed because most Americans don't understand geography anyway.

The Philippines plays its usual historical, pivotal role by dropping leaflets all over the Swiss countryside, which show white Europeans getting a massage in Manila that is so good, only their heels and the back of their heads are touching the table. The Swiss, also always looking for a good time, invade the Philippines but are quickly overwhelmed by the unified force of the other Gang of Eight, which is able to strike from neighboring Thailand with lightening speed. I don't know who won either, but these groups don't care either.

The Nada Grata's League (NGL)

As the name implies, this league pretty much represents the "down south/no thanks league." The Far Center just isn't high on this league's ability to mount anything on a global, military-threat basis. In addition, nobody wants to go there, much less invade it, because they always get the runs after their first meal. I don't know about you, but I didn't do anything but just **read** a book about Mexico once, and had to spend a week in the toilet recovering. I'm not going there, and nobody else is either.

Even if conquering armies survived the "trots," what do they get for all their brain damage? Exactamundo, Nada! A currency that is totally useless; dictators like the former Hugo Chávez, who made everybody in Venezuela turn their clocks back one-half hour—if you can believe that crap; women in Bolivia who wear men's hats and look just like idiots; and Peru, who elected as one of their Presidents a Japanese, for the love of Christ, and so on and so forth.

For a continent that covers roughly 20 percent of the earth's landmass, South America occupies about 2 percent of everybody's attention. Enough said. They'll be on the sidelines watching, if they wake up from the siesta in time.

The "Stans" Around League (SAL)

Excellent, reader. You nailed this one right away. Turkmeni**stan**, Paki**stan**, Afghani**stan**, Kurdi**stan**, Kazakh**stan**, Uzbeki**stan**, Tajiki**stan**, and my all-time favorite that nobody can pronounce, nobody knows where it is, nobody knows what it does, nobody knows how it came into being, and, definitely, nobody cares about **Kyrgyzstan**.

You may be asking yourself, "If I don't know about these 'stans' (or whatever they are), and nobody else does either, then why are you putting them in planetary, pugilistic play?" Simple: They are in a rebuilding mode and could prove to be players within the three- to five-year timeframe. They're balanced, poised, overlooked, underrated, and have a lock on the only thing more powerful than oil––dope! Yeah, baby. These robe-wearing, cave-dwelling, hygienically challenged rascals have more poppies then you can shake a stick at. And "poppy" makes heroine, and heroine is dope, and the world is wild about this stuff. Not only do they have the raw material (poppies), but these guys have marketing savvy well beyond their years.

They will employ the Jafia marketing technique. The simplicity and effectiveness of this approach is stunning. Jafia is a combination of the words Japan and Mafia. Kind of a new-age East-meets-West marketing arrangement. Step 1: Flood the market with high-grade, non-unionized, primo smack at Wal-Mart affordability prices. This is the Japan side of the equation. Step 2: Kill anybody who gets in your way. This is the mob side of the equation.

Look for these guys to be "odds-on" in the 2020/2021 season. Don't say I didn't tell you!

The League of Their Own League (LOTOL)

Using my very best voice, **will the Magnificent Seven please step forward and do so in alphabetical order?**

- Australia
- China
- Great Britain

- India
- Japan
- Russia
- United States

Seventy percent of the earth's land mass; 95 percent of the world's wealth; 99 percent of the planet's military might; Muslim muzzling; nation building; terrorist hating; good ole boys with balls the size of a Brahman bull.

Alternative One:

They've got it all! But how do we keep the Magnificent Seven from making a Magnificent Mess by annihilating each other? **Are we called the Far Center for a reason?** It's so obvious Al Gore could get it. Seven countries, seven continents—bingo. Just divvy the world up. Australia can have Australia, since it's a continent and they wouldn't have to screw around relocating all those aborigines to a new place where they could screw over them again. The United States stays put and occupies North **and** South America, since Canada has done an abysmal job with a country that is 3,000 miles long and half a mile wide, and all those "Nada Gratas" to the south, discussed earlier, haven't exactly set the world on fire either. Also, the U.S. wouldn't have to screw around relocating all those American Indians to a new place where they could screw over them again. You get the idea, and a damn fine one it is, too!

Alternative Two:

What a coincidence again! We're talking about the PCS being like the American Football BCS, right? Guess what the BCS has that the PCS needs? Seven umpires to officiate the game, right? Guess how many umps there are in a college football game. Good God, y'all...it's heaven sent. The Magnificent Seven become the Seven PCS umpires.

In order to ensure that nobody gets their nose bent out of shape, each country will rotate between the seven umpire positions each year. Those positions are: 1) referee Buddha, 2) umpire Pope, 3) head linesman Yahweh, 4) line judge Dali, 5) field judge Orthodox anything, 6) side judge Ghandi, and 7) back judge Dante.

We, in the Far Center believe this concept, will, over time, not only catch on but cost the world $20 billion to administer and morph to a new name called The United Nations. What do **you** think?

Alternative Three:

All wars are fought online. China's got this down pat already.

FROM THE AUTHOR

Whether you are a limp-wristed Liberal or a Clinch-fisted Conservative, try strengthening your wrist and opening your hand and at the least learn how to say "up yours" politely!

Printed in the United States
By Bookmasters